PERFECTIONISM

A Practical Guide to Managing
"NEVER GOOD ENOUGH"

LISA VAN GEMERT
M.Ed.T.

Book layout design by saqib_arshad

ISBN 9781793867674

Printed in the United States of America

Who better to write a book about perfectionism than a recovering perfectionist? Lisa Van Gemert is just that person. She offers invaluable new insights on perfectionism as a tendency and not a label which enables smart strategies for those debilitated by its multi-faceted nature and real-life consequences. It is a must-read for parents and teachers struggling to understand the young perfectionists in their lives.

~ Lisa Conrad, Owner, Gifted Parenting Support, and Moderator of Global #gtchat Powered by TAGT on Twitter.

Lisa Van Gemert is your guide out of Perfectionland! She intimately knows the challenges of perfectionism and gives inspiration and a roadmap for a life filled with joy, while still pursuing your personal best. The stories and strategies in these pages can literally transform lives and allow those you care about to accept who they are and live fully while embracing life's journey.

~ Dan Peters, Ph.D. Clinical Psychologist and co-founder of Summit Center, and author of *Make Your Worrier a Warrior: A Guide to Conquering Your Child's Fears* and related books.

Van Gemert draws on diverse theories and narratives and offers refreshing insight to our understanding perfectionism. The strategies and models for managing perfectionism in this book could be life-changing.

~ Todd Kettler, Ph.D., College of Education. University of North Texas

This book was a pleasure to read. The examples Lisa used all felt like people I know. Lisa Van Gemert's examples felt very familiar, which was a tremendous comfort. I wish I had known these strategies in raising my own highly capable children. Her suggestions make good sense for busy parents and teachers who might find that some of the ideas would be useful for themselves.

I have already begun using ideas from this book and have recommended it to others. This will be a truly useful addition to my classroom library. Full of commonsense advice for parents and teachers, and a good helping of humor, the logical strategies will be easy to try at home and at school. It reads like a conversation with a wise friend who understands how perfectionists struggle and knows how to translate ideas into action.

~ Jane Hesslein, M.A., Humanities teacher, Seattle Country Day School and former Board member, Supporting Emotional Needs of Gifted

DEDICATION

For Steve
Thank you for being the president of my fan club. Ewigkeit.

ACKNOWLEDGMENTS

I'll never forget the day that Dr. James Webb told me he'd heard a SENGinar I'd done on perfectionism and ended with, "Have you thought of writing a book?" I don't think I fully appreciated that he was serious until, somehow, I found myself working on a manuscript. In addition to Jim's early belief in me, confidence I still feel amazed by, I was helped by the confidence and encouragement of so many others.

At the very real risk of neglecting someone, I would like to acknowledge some of the generous help I have been given that made it possible to bring this book to fruition.

My best friend, Patti Bear, read the first tentative chapters with a keen eye. A therapist, she kept me honest and on track where my ideas brushed up against mental health issues. Mistakes are mine; accuracies are hers. Laurie Westphal, author, colleague, and friend, figuratively held my hand through the entire process, sharing ideas, suggestions, feedback, and support. Luckily, cell phones have unlimited minutes now, or I would owe her hundreds of dollars in phone bills in addition to my gratitude.

I have learned at the feet of so many greats, including most notably Dr. Dan Peters and Dr. Ed Amend. In my opinion, these two men are titans in the world of giftedness, especially our gifted children who suffer. It was in a professional development with them that I knew I wanted to do more than learn; I wanted to contribute.

There would have been no book had there been no students, for that is where I learned what worked (and often what didn't). My own children,

Gregory, Jonathan, and Joseph, are witnesses to my most stunning imperfections, yet they have been a well of support that has never run dry.

Abraham Lincoln famously said, "All that I am every am or hope to be I owe to my angel mother." I will borrow those words to use for my own mother, Margaret Ross, a woman of incredible strength and determination who raised me to believe that I could and should do something worthwhile with every good gift and talent I was given. She can also tell a story like nobody's business, and I've tried to learn her art.

It is my great sadness that my beloved grandmother, Laura Gates Morey, died just before the publication of this book. She never graduated from high school, leaving her education during the Depression to help her mother provide for thirteen children she was raising alone. She was enormously proud that her granddaughter was going to write a "real" book. Her daily phone conversations, each one beginning, "Hello, Sweetheart!" kept me going on very long days.

Lastly, there are simply not words to describe my gratitude to my husband, Steven Van Gemert. He has not only given me this amazingly fun last name, but he is the self-proclaimed president of my fan club and my rock. Every crazy idea I've had, he's supported. Without him, there would be no book, nor any number of the amazing blessings I have in my life. We share our family, our struggles, our joys, and our commitment to God, and I owe him a debt of gratitude I can never repay.

TABLE OF CONTENTS

A Native of Perfectionland

It is no surprise that I have written a book on Perfectionism. I come by my understanding of it honestly, having struggled with it most of my life. I am a Perfectionland native, having grown up on its troubled shores, though I could not have defined or named the feeling inside me as perfectionism. I didn't even think of it as trying to be perfect or trying to be the best. I just thought of it as trying to be okay, to be as good as everyone else. I know now that my perfectionism came from a deep feeling of emptiness and unworthiness. I have come to realize this pattern is a frequent one for perfectionists, and that bright young people are especially prone to perfectionism due in part to their idealism.

I have written this book for fellow perfectionists with the hope it will give them ways to mitigate harmful thoughts and behavior patterns that make up the phenomenon called perfectionism. In addition, I hope that parents and teachers, especially those with bright, talented students, will be able to use the information and strategies in the various chapters to help children who are showing symptoms of perfectionism.in their classrooms and homes each day.

For a long time, I thought the inner loneliness I felt was because I was an only child. I pretended I had brothers and sisters, and I deeply envied my friends who did have them. How I longed to be a member of the large, happy Partridge Family. I wanted to be Tracy, the youngest child, because I knew I would feel so safe and so much a part of something if only I were the youngest child in a big family. Years later, I came to realize that it wasn't about being an only child, but rather about never feeling like I belonged.

Looking back, I realize the habits I thought everyone had were not typical for most people. In elementary school, I kept track of all of my grades in my Trapper Keeper binder. I would feel a rise of panic if I received a grade lower than an A on any assignment, and eventually, I decided it would be best to make sure I never got a grade lover than ninety-three because then I would stay safely away from B territory. If I were worried that I couldn't do well in a class, I would drop it. I dropped Advanced Placement English during the second semester to take *Myths and Legends* instead because I knew I could have the best grade in that class. I carefully orchestrated my life, so much so that I even made a deal with my high school counselor: if I came to the end of the semester in Calculus and I had less than an A, I could drop the class, even on the last day.

Even now, I still have a recurring nightmare—one I've had since high school—that it is the end of the semester and I have to take a final exam, yet I haven't gone to the class all semester and know nothing about it. When I was in college, my perfectionism prompted me to churn through majors like milk in an ice cream machine. I toyed with being a doctor, a lawyer, an astronomer, and even a flight attendant! If I encountered a class where I thought I could not get an A, I dropped the class and fled the major. Organic chemistry, Logic, Calculus, and more were all dropped on the last possible day.

My expectations of others were as high as the ones I had for myself, and as a result, I struggled to maintain friendships. A common quality of bright children is wanting more intimate relationships earlier than their peers, and that was true for me, but my expectations were simply too high and too intense. I wanted people to be my best friend and to forsake all others, and I expected them to be as idealistic and concerned with quality as I was. I tried to move friendships forward too quickly. I bounced from one group of people to another, never really fitting in anywhere. Not surprisingly, others did not reciprocate my attempts at friendship. I remember my mother's giving me a wonderful party for my sixteenth birthday, and I invited lots of classmates, but only a couple of people came.

I was too intense, too picky, and too uptight to be someone with whom people wanted to spend time. Even being a cheerleader didn't save me from social suicide. I practiced to be very good at the skills, but I struggled to get along with the others. For years, I blamed the other girls. However, the truth is that I was incredibly difficult to get along with, as I wanted everything to be perfect and idyllic, like it was in the books I devoured.

I didn't just struggle to have normal relationships; I also didn't find pleasure in the activities many other kids enjoyed. I refused to go meet Michael Jackson when I was a young girl because I was doing something else I thought was more important. That was just one example of how I missed out on things because I was hyper-focused on a task.

When playing with my Barbies˙ at about age 8 or 9, I never actually played with the dolls themselves. I just arranged their things in beautiful order. I would spend all of my play time setting it all up, making everything just so. I did the same thing with toy cars. I spent one Christmas afternoon totally cleaning and rearranging my room to make sure all of my new toys fit in well and my room organization system still worked. I thought everyone behaved this way.

It wasn't just grades and toys. It was my weight as well. In tenth grade, during a unit on the digestive system, my Anatomy and Physiology teacher had us track everything we ate for a week. I remember turning my record in and being shocked when she called me in to talk about it. She said,

"Have you ever heard the word 'anorexia'?" I wasn't anorexic, I told her. I ate. In fact, I was fat. How could I be fat *and* anorexic? I was 5'4" and weighed one hundred and two pounds. That was nearly obese, in my opinion. Someone had told me not long before that I was "hippy," and I was trying hard to make sure I didn't get any heavier. I thought that eating lettuce with vinegar on it for lunch was normal. In order to avoid eating dinner, I would say I wasn't hungry. If I did eat, I exercised it off. I played soccer. I was a cheerleader. I swam. I exercised in my room if I didn't have something organized to do. My teacher referred me to the counselor, and I was able to recover from the anorexia, but it was just one more manifestation of the perfectionism that tormented me. A nearly constant sense of dissatisfaction hovered over me like the little gray cloud hovering over Eeyore.

Deciding to Write This Book

A favorite part of my job these days is speaking to parent groups. I love sharing ideas with them, and I especially enjoy when they bring their kids along. One of the most popular sessions I do is a workshop on perfectionism. At the end of the session, parents often ask me if there is a book they could read that could help them assist their children who are struggling with perfectionism. They, themselves, also often are struggling with it, and they are desperate to spare their children the pain it caused— and sometimes still causes—them. I saw a need for a book that talked about perfectionism from the perspective of bright, gifted children.

I call perfectionism an occupational hazard of giftedness because if you interact with gifted children or adults for any length of time, I guarantee you will encounter perfectionists. As an educator (yes, I finally settled on a major and became a teacher), I have observed students struggling with many of the same situations and concerns that robbed me of so much enjoyment when I was a child. My heart aches when children as young as five years old share stories with me that are hauntingly familiar to my own. I can see the future that lies before them, and I want to help them.

It is incredibly rewarding to have educators who have participated in my training tell me that the strategies they learned helped them make a difference in children's lives. Throughout my career, I've worked with thousands of students, teachers, and parents. However, writing this book allows me to share with a wider audience in the hope that the information will help others avoid the pitfalls I encountered on my own Perfectionland journey.

Perfectionism not only drains life of its joy, but also feeds other mental health conditions that can debilitate children, teenagers, and adults. Perfectionism is best friends with anxiety and depression, and even when it is not completely incapacitating, perfectionism can rob life of some of its greatest joys. It's exhausting to try to be perfect and to maintain impossibly high standards. It can ruin a childhood in many ways and have unintended consequences. I was blessed to have a teacher who intervened to save my health, but it could easily have ended very differently.

The silver lining is that the negative effects of perfectionism can be mitigated. We can understand it better and develop strategies to manage it. It can become a part of our past, not our present or future. We can learn to set high, but reasonable, standards. We can learn to become satisfied with our efforts and be kinder to ourselves. Perfectionism is, at its essence, the search for excellence in the absence of self-love. We can learn to seek excellence in the presence of self-love. We can build our children's (and our own) resistance to the pressures of perfectionism.

Am I still a perfectionist? No, I would say that I'm not. I like things neat, and I set high standards for myself, but I no longer suffer from the negative effects of perfectionism. I have strategies I use to calm the voice in my head that says I'm not good enough. It is my sincere hope that the information in this book can help others to have healthier relationships with themselves and thus become foreigners in Perfectionland.

About This Book

This book blends theory and practice to help parents and educators understand perfectionism in a way that empowers them to help children with whom they live and work. It is also designed to help perfectionists move beyond perfectionism in their own lives. Many of the stories and examples can be shared with children to facilitate discussion. In fact, if the child is about twelve years old, or older, I encourage you to share the entire book with him or her. Its ultimate purpose is to help people rediscover the joy of living life free of the shackles of perfectionism, and to find satisfaction and happiness rather than frustration and despair.

Every chapter of the book includes Action Steps for readers to take to help apply the knowledge and skills in practical ways. I have written the book in a conversational way, imagining that you were sitting with me in my family room, chatting on the couch. I have kept in my mind's eye the image of some of the parents and children with whom I've worked in the past, and if you're reading this book, you are, in a very real way, my friend.

Through the power of story, the description of strategies, and the explanation of various aspects of perfectionism, you will learn about perfectionism and how to counteract its effects. You will learn about the negative impact of perfectionism, discovering that it isn't always easy to detect and not always to blame. You will understand how to avoid setting up a climate of perfectionism, whether you are a parent or an educator. You will discover strategies for mitigating its effects, and you will appreciate how parents and teachers can have a powerful positive effect on youth struggling with perfectionism. By the time you finish the book, you will know the role of resilience, failure, motivation, and self-concept in tackling perfectionism.

Why am I sure this book is worth your time? Because the girl I was in school long ago is not the person I am today, and I've used these ideas and strategies to help many children and parents develop a healthier relationship with the expectations that go with high ability. I've seen young people smile when they earned an eighty-three on a paper, walking away from my desk with a sense of deep satisfaction. I've had parents email me about changes they've made within their families to make it less likely that their children will grow up in a perfectionism Petri dish.

I hope you will use this book as a starting point for discussion with the youth in your life. I also hope this book can be a guide to help you if perfectionism is getting in the way of your happiness or preventing you from being able to positively model how to have high standards without the misery that can accompany excessive perfectionism.

While I have relied on information from trained and licensed mental health professionals, this book is not to be used in place of counseling or therapy. Please seek help from a qualified professional if you feel that it would be useful to you or your child. I have come to believe strongly in the power of professional help. It can be expensive, I know, yet I also believe it can be an investment that pays tremendous dividends. If you do see a counselor, you can discuss the ideas and strategies in this book with him or her so that you can implement the most effective and appropriate strategies for your situation.

Ready to leave Perfectionland? Let's get going!

A New Paradigm for Perfectionism

Perfectionism is not a quest for the best. It is a pursuit of the worst in ourselves, the part that tells us that nothing we do will ever be good enough—that we should try again.

\- JULIA CAMERON

What is the worst punishment you can imagine? In Greek mythology, the story of Sisyphus illustrates what the gods thought was ultimate torment. Sisyphus was the king of Corinth, and by all accounts, he was not a great guy. His list of sins and misdeeds could fill its own book, and when he offended both Zeus and Hades, he was condemned to an eternal punishment. Sent to Tartarus, the lowest region of the Underworld, Sisyphus was required to roll a massive boulder to the top of a steep hill. The problem was that as Sisyphus neared the top of the mountain, the rock would roll back down again. Sisyphus would then have to begin to push it to the top once more, only to see it roll back down yet one more time. To the Greeks, doing the same fruitless labor over and over was torment.

While very few people spend their days literally rolling boulders to the tops of mountains only to watch them roll back down, many people do this figuratively. We call that fruitless effort *perfectionism.* The truth is that even if you want to be perfect, you can't be. It's a cliché to say that nobody is perfect, and one of the things that makes perfectionism so damaging is that we like to tell our children "you can be anything you want to be," but we forget to mention that "perfect isn't one of the choices." You simply cannot be perfect, no matter how hard you try. So, kids or adults who are focused on trying to be perfect will almost always feel dissatisfaction, depression, and anxiety as they constantly seek something that's unattainable. They become the emotional equivalent of Sisyphus, always struggling, yet never satisfied.

Perfectionism is characterized as setting impossibly high standards and striving for flawlessness, combined with excessive self-criticism, an unhealthy concern for others' opinions of one's work, and overgeneralization of failure despite adverse consequences. Let's separate these parts out: setting impossibly high standards, *and* trying to be flawless, *and* being too hard on oneself, *and* being very concerned about what other people think, *and* typically thinking that failing at something is indicative of pervasive worthlessness, *and* it's hurting you.

When you break it apart like this, you can see that it takes several factors in order for perfectionism to be problematic. If you have high standards, but you don't care what other people think and you're not too hard on yourself when you don't attain those standards, it's unlikely that perfectionism is causing real difficulty for you. Essentially, perfectionism boils down to unreasonable expectations of oneself combined with a lack of self-love. As one colleague said, "Perfectionism is like cholesterol; there's good cholesterol and bad cholesterol." There is nothing wrong with setting high standards; the problems arise when it causes you misery and interferes with your life.

A Changing Paradigm of Perfectionism

A common view of perfectionism is thinking of it as a dichotomy: you're either a perfectionist or you're not. This all-or-nothing view adds to the defeatism that often follows perfectionists around like a little grey cloud over their heads. In his book on perfectionism written especially for kids, psychologist Thomas Greenspon, explained:

> *Perfectionism might feel like something that is 'wrong with you' – like a disease you should get rid of, and once you do you'll be perfect. But easing the burden of perfectionism is not about getting rid of something bad. It's about learning to judge yourself less harshly and learning to find ways to feel acceptable.*[1]

It also lends itself to the idea that in order to avoid the negative consequences of perfectionism, you have to rid yourself of it completely. When you are unsuccessful in this, you get discouraged, throw up your hands, and say, "I can't help it! I'm just a perfectionist!"

I'd like to suggest a new way of thinking about perfectionism. I believe that perfectionism, like most things, is a continuum. Imagine in your mind the standard bell curve. In some areas of our lives, we will be to the left of the curve in our perfectionistic tendencies, sloppy or haphazard. In other areas, we may be much more meticulous, perhaps to the point that it's causing us problems. Very few people are all the way to the right of the perfectionism bell curve in every aspect of their lives. Rather, they move back and forth along the continuum, sometimes even changing the things about which they are perfectionistic.

Here's an example. Nine-year-old LeDarion, is remarkably perfectionistic in most areas of his life. At school, his pencils are all sharpened to within an inch of their lives; he won't turn in work until he believes it could be used as an example for years to come; and he struggles not to have a tantrum when he receives a grade less than 100%. His teacher has asked the counselor to evaluate LeDarion's perfectionism because he feels like it's causing LeDarion to be anxious at school. Yet anyone seeing LeDarion's room at home would find it difficult to believe that his teacher's greatest worry about him is his paralyzing perfectionism. To call his bedroom a mess would be an understatement; he has no real standard or concern for it in the same way he cares about his assignments being perfect, or the need to maintain structure at school.

For kids like LeDarion, the unevenness of the perfectionism often confuses adults around them. If perfectionism is situational, then people not associated with that situation may not realize the extent of the problem. I see this often with homework when a child will try and try to get it perfect, working for hours at the kitchen table, frustration growing on the part of everyone in the household. The teacher, however, is unaware because the teacher never sees the child struggling in that situation.

For most things in life, the majority of us are in the middle of the bell curve, though we vary depending on the situation. We set a standard for ourselves in hygiene (our clothes are clean, we shower regularly), cleanliness (we take out trash, we vacuum), or professionalism (we show up to work or school on time, we meet deadlines). Very few people are equal opportunity perfectionists or perfectionistic in every single area of their life. This can make it hard to understand because the same kid who is neurotically perfectionistic about schoolwork may be, like LeDarion, the complete opposite in taking care of his bedroom or personal things at home.

This confusion can be even more striking in kids who have executive functioning issues. The same child who struggled for hours at the kitchen table may not turn the work in, finding the path from the backpack to the teacher's inbox an impossible abyss. Children who suffer from ADHD or other disorders are likely to show inconsistent standards and follow through in their behaviors, and often are perplexed and distraught as to why they can't be organized like others.

So, as we embark on an exploration of perfectionism and how to manage it, the first of the two truths we're going to start with is that you're never going to be perfect. This realization can create its own difficulties as we come to understand and accept that. Those of us who were expecting to find a cure have to accept that it may be a chronic condition for us—treatable, but not curable. Secondly, you're not necessarily going to possess the same level of perfectionism in all areas of your life. Just because your backpack looks like the bomb squad did a test explosion in it doesn't mean you aren't struggling with perfectionism. Because of this, I prefer not to label people perfectionists, but rather to say that they have perfectionistic tendencies or that they strive for perfection.

Connection to Underachievement

Sometimes people who demonstrate perfectionism get so frustrated by their inability to be perfect that they go the complete opposite direction. I live in Texas, and it gets very hot in Texas in the summer. Trust me, the last place you want to be during the summer in Texas is in an attic. Unfortunately, one year we had to clean our attic during the summer in preparation for a new roof, and to psych ourselves up for the task, my husband and I watched an episode of the television show *Hoarders*. It was perfect motivational therapy for cleaning the attic or the garage, even in the middle of the summer. It made us want to throw away everything we own.

In the show, the characters discussed the origins of the person's perfectionism. They asked the woman, who was the hoarder, what she thought put her on the road that led toward hoarding. She replied, "Well, I was a perfectionist." My husband snorted in disbelief. How could someone whose house looked like that be a perfectionist? How could you go from being a perfectionist to being unable to walk across a room in your house? That's hard for most people to understand, yet I totally understood it.

Often if you're seeking perfectionism and you realize you can't get there (remember Sisyphus?), your frustration leads you toward the complete opposite side of the spectrum. Sometimes, kids struggling with perfectionism who find they cannot be perfect in school don't slide into the A minus or B range, but instead go into F mode, which can be particularly damaging. But it's important to understand that perfectionism can often be the root of some people's failures or look like they lack concern for their success. If we interpret this failure as laziness or rebellion, we may approach the student's underachievement in the entirely wrong way.

I'll be describing strategies for managing perfectionism later in the book, but it's important to understand the working theory behind them. My best friend is a counselor in private practice who specializes in counseling the gifted, and she said to me one time, "Your theory guides your intervention." When I asked her to elaborate, she said, "If you're a teacher and a student isn't doing her homework, and your theory is that she doesn't understand how to do it, your intervention and how you deal with that will be different from your intervention if your theory is that she is lazy." My theory is that people who lean toward perfectionism can grow to have a healthier relationship with it if they are encouraged to nudge themselves back towards the middle of the bell curve, rather than thinking in black and white terms of "I'm either a perfectionist or I'm not." That theory will guide my suggested interventions.

Types of Perfectionism

Perfectionism comes in a few fabulous flavors, some more common than others. One discussion of different types of perfectionism is described in *Letting Go of Perfect* (Adelson & Wilson, 2009).[2]. The first face of perfectionism is the *Academic Overachiever*. These kids *have* to get 100% on every assignment, or the world is going to come to a grinding halt. If they earn a score of ninety-eight, they go into the teacher's room after school, walk up to the desk and demand, "Why did I get a ninety-eight?" This question is quickly followed by, "Do you give extra credit?" This is the most common kind of perfectionism that we see in the classroom. This kind of perfectionism can look like arrogance or over-developed competitiveness, making the child seem less likeable, rather than suffering.

A second type of perfectionist is the *Aggravated Accuracy Assessor*. These are the people who have in their minds the way the task should look in the ideal world, and they get frustrated when they can't drag and drop it from their minds to the paper in the way they imagined it. When I taught third grade, I would see these kids sometimes erase and erase and erase until they literally wore a hole in the paper. My eleventh-grade student, David, was so debilitated by this type of perfectionism that he was unable to pass the state-mandated English test. He had gone so far in this type of perfectionism that he couldn't write an essay without using Wite-Out° tape to cover up words and phrases he felt were unworthy. Because Wite-Out wasn't allowed during the test, he felt paralyzed, unable to move forward. Eventually, we had to get him an accommodation to use Wite-Out.

This type of perfectionism is not limited to children. Adults sometimes repeat tasks over and over and over again to the point where the tasks don't get done at all. I call it *Pinterest Perfectionism*, named for the social media channel that can create unreasonable expectations if we set it as a standard. Pinterest shows us a finished product resulting from hours (even days or weeks) spent on a single task, and then perfectly photographed. An individual struggling with Pinterest Perfectionism thinks he or she should do *everything* to the level that the Pinterest person did this *one thing*, and should be able to do it on the first try. Social media isn't the only problem, though. We go to parties or school events and see everyone else with clean, compliant children, thinking of the struggle we had just to get out the door, our own children wolfing down peanut butter and jelly sandwiches in the car on the way. Those with Pinterest Perfectionism compare their everyday normal to others' perceived perfection without considering the work or struggle they endured. If our efforts aren't as perfect, we feel we have failed.

This can be problematic in the workplace and even lead to job loss. It can create unhealthy levels of competition, as we believe we must consistently do better than what has been done by others. We feel threatened by others' success, which makes us less of a team player.

Risk Evaders, as described by Adelson and Wilson, are afraid to take a risk and give up if they don't get it right the first time. This is particularly damaging because risk taking is necessary for growth. If they don't take risks, by trying things that don't come easily to them, they will never grow. For gifted kids this often is a problem because so many things do come easily to them. At school, these kids stick to tasks they know they can do well, but do not expand their skill set because virtually every assignment offers an option that doesn't require extension beyond their current level of mastery. To grow, there must be risk to try new things and experience challenges.

Risk evasion extends beyond the walls of the school. It can happen in sports, in fine arts, and can creep into areas that don't seem like achievement domains, such trying a new book author or genre of books. Ten-year-old Emily was devoted to the *Redwall* series and refused to explore another series, preferring to read books she knew rather than embark on the unknown. "Emily," I suggested, "if you like *Redwall*, I think you may like the *Chronicles of Prydain* series as well. Have you tried those?"

"No, but I'll go read about them and decide," she answered. Her elaborate ritual for deciding to read a new book included reading every review on Amazon and Goodreads, even if there were hundreds of them, and then mastering the names and relationships among the characters. Then, and only then, would she read the book. "I want to be able to answer questions if someone sees me with the book," she explained. Her parents saw her as a budding literary critic, but I saw her as a risk evader, determined to be a master, never an apprentice.

Another kind of perfectionist, the *Controlling Image Manager*, is particularly concerned with the persona that they've created for themselves. They think, "This is who I want people to believe that I am," and often at the core of that self-image is the idea of being a bright, talented, gifted individual. This type is intricately interwoven with Impostor Syndrome, the fear or feeling that if you cannot do everything perfectly, then you're not really gifted, and someone eventually will find you out. You will be revealed as powerless and fraudulent like the Wizard of Oz or the Emperor with no clothes.

Controlling Image Managers often worry others will perceive them as less than smart academically, but it can be a problem in other domains as well. Those who are in fine arts may have an internal dialogue that says, "It is crucial that people see me as a talented actor (or musician or painter)." The drive to maintain their image is so important that some Controlling Image Managers pretend they don't want something, even if they do, in order to preserve the persona. They'll say, "Well, I don't even want to try out for the school play. I could be the lead if I tried out, but I don't even want to try out." In actuality, they deeply would like to be in the play, but they're worried that they're not going to get the lead. If they don't get the lead, but rather some supporting role, people's view of them might change. They worry that *everybody* will be sitting in the audience saying, "How come he's not the lead this time? I think he was the lead last time. I guess he's not as good as he thought. I guess he's not good at all." In that way, the self-talk of the Controlling Image Manager goes down a rabbit hole of persona implosion that has the same effect as risk evasion—the loss of opportunity. The difference between the two types is the audience. Risk Evaders suffer from a fear-based concern for their view of themselves, while Controlling Image Managers struggle with a more existential worry about others' view of them and their own innate worthiness.

Next are the *Procrastinating Perfectionists* who have a complicated relationship with some fairly simple math. They think that a zero you earned when you didn't turn in the work is better than an eighty you earned when you did turn in the work. Why? Because with the zero there's always a possibility that *if* they had turned it in, they would have gotten a one hundred, whereas with the eighty that possibility is gone forever. An eighty is a B, in fact it's almost a C, and so that's *horrible*. The Procrastinating Perfectionist thinks, not necessarily at the top of consciousness, "It's better to get the zero and keep in my mind the idea that I maybe could have had a high grade; I would have gotten a hundred if I had turned it in. I could have had it if I had tried."

Procrastinating perfectionism is a common reason that gifted kids' performance in school often doesn't match their ability. Teachers end up with a grade book that looks like Swiss cheese. The row of grades will be: one hundred, one hundred, one hundred, zero, zero, zero, one hundred, one hundred, zero, zero, zero, zero. It is difficult for the adults around the student to understand what is going on. It boils down to an inability to complete the task in the way that you feel like you could or should, and this gets compounded with habits of procrastination.

In classrooms, this type of perfectionism is the kind that often most confuses us. We see kids with tremendous ability, yet their grades do not accurately represent that ability. One student, Rochelle, completely confused her teacher, Mr. Waterston, when she didn't turn in a big project on an Asian country. What confused him was that Rochelle had been so passionate about the project. She had selected her country, South Korea, and had talked with him several times over the course of the project about her plans. Her excitement seemed genuine, so he was completely surprised when she turned nothing in the day the projects were due.

He asked to speak with her after class, and she just shrugged in response to his question about why she hadn't turned in the work.

Mr. Waterston called Rochelle's parents, who expressed equal confusion. They had taken her to buy supplies for the project, and were shocked she didn't turn it in. Her father's finding her shredded poster board in the recycling bin finally led to a tearful explanation; she was so frustrated with her inability to make a project that matched in execution her passion for the topic that she felt unworthy of creating anything. She felt she would be letting down the entire nation of South Korea if she turned in a second-rate project. Mr. Waterston's assurances meant nothing to her, and Rochelle could not be persuaded to turn the project in late, even for full credit. The situation sparked a tumbling cascade of negative effects on her performance in class, as the impact of a zero for a test grade led to discouragement and a lack of incentive to try in other, smaller assignments. One of the brightest students in the class, Rochelle barely passed the class that grading period.

Do any of these types of perfectionism resonate with you? Are you realizing that a child you didn't think was perfectionistic actually is? Perfectionism is a chameleon whose changing colors and types often camouflage its presence. These types of perfectionism are not exhaustive, and you may have witnessed or even struggled with other manifestations of perfectionism.

Perfectionism Isn't Always What It Seems

When Ethan started school, everything was fine for a while. One day during third grade, he brought home directions for an assigned science project. When his parents looked at the instructions, his dad, an astrophysicist, got a brilliant idea for the project Ethan might do. He tried to describe it to Ethan, but it was a little above Ethan's ability. Eventually, dad ended up doing quite a bit more of the project than was appropriate. The completed project looked terrific, in no small part because of the over-involvement of Ethan's dad.

The next time Ethan's teacher gave him a project to do, this time in Language Arts, he barely gave the instructions a glance. Ethan brought it home and handed it to his dad. This time, his dad told Ethan he needed to do the project himself. Because the last project, done in large part by his dad, looked terrific, Ethan became extremely frustrated with and frightened by what he would need to do by himself. He knew what he would turn in for this assignment looked very different from his last project, and he was embarrassed. His parents, noticing his frustration and knowing how common perfectionism is among the gifted, assumed that Ethan was struggling with perfectionism, rather than struggling with living up to an impossibly high standard set by an over-involved parent.

As time went on, Ethan learned that he could get extra help from his parents by showing frustration with assignments. His parents, blaming his perfectionism and trying to reduce what they perceived as anxiety arising from it, stepped in over and over. Inadvertently, they created a situation where a child appeared to be a perfectionist, when in actuality he was a fearful procrastinator. By the time Ethan was in high school, he was completely habituated to procrastinating assignments, his parents were habituated to making excuses and over-involving themselves, and Ethan had learned that the word "perfectionism" was a get-out-of-schoolwork-free card.

Because perfectionism is so common among bright children, sometimes we stop there when trying to determine what is causing a child to have issues with schoolwork. While Ethan's parents meant well and couldn't see where the road they embarked on with that science project would lead, they inadvertently ended up with their child's being labeled a perfectionist, when in actuality he may not have been. We should be careful in labeling a child a perfectionist, as the child can adopt that as part of his or her identity when it otherwise would not be.

Perfectionism as an Aspect of Personality

One reason I resist labeling people perfectionists, preferring to say they have perfectionistic tendencies or struggle with perfectionism, is because calling someone a perfectionist creates a very narrow concept of their personality. Perfectionism is just one of many aspects of personality found on personality model inventories. The Big Five personality traits model,[3] for example, identifies perfectionism as an extreme form of the factor *conscientiousness*. In this model, conscientiousness is described as a tendency toward organization and dependability. People with low conscientiousness can look lazy, disorganized, unreliable, or sloppy, while people with high conscientiousness look super organized and reliable. Viewed in a slightly different way, this highlights the connection between perfectionism and what we would call executive functioning skills—the ability to manage one's life.

People with strong executive functioning skills not only plan and do their work before it is due, they also turn it in on time. They meet deadlines, have necessary supplies, and manage time effectively. You can see how, taken to the extreme, this could land you in a somewhat obsessive place, desperately concerned about not being able to do these things. With or without the Big Five model, it can be helpful to see perfectionism as an extreme manifestation of otherwise normal behavior.

Key Ideas

- Perfectionism is not an either/or situation, and people can be perfectionistic in some areas of their life but not others.
- Perfectionism comes in different types, and individuals may manifest perfectionism in many ways.
- Perfectionism can actually be a factor in underachievement.
- Procrastination and perfectionism can co-exist.
- Perfectionism can be managed, not necessarily cured.
- Perfectionism often is a normal aspect of personality gone awry.

Action Steps

- List some areas of your life and your child's life such as school/work, chores, personal appearance/hygiene, etc. Using a bell curve drawing, mark where you each feel you are in different areas of your life with regard to perfectionism.
- Discuss Adelson and Wilson's types of perfectionism with the child. Explore the types of perfectionism that resonate with the child, and share what types of perfectionism resonate with you about yourself.
- Discuss characters from films, books, and social media who demonstrate perfectionistic tendencies. Include in the discussion whether the perfectionism is helping the person or not.4
- Break large projects for school or home into smaller, manageable steps, and mark the progress towards the completion of the project.

The Dramatic Downside of Perfectionism

CHAPTER II

The pursuit of perfection often impedes improvement.

\- GEORGE WILL

One day at a PTA meeting, Joshua's mother, Angela, heard about an upcoming birthday party for a long-time friend of his, but she knew her son had not been invited to the party. When she got home, she asked Joshua about it. After a long conversation fraught with tears and evasion, Angela discovered the birthday boy, Elijah, was no longer a friend. Since Elijah's mom was a fairly good friend, Angela called her to ask about the end of the friendship because she felt Joshua was hiding something from her.

Elijah's mother gently explained that Elijah had begun to feel uncomfortable around Joshua because of Joshua's insistence on exactness when the two boys were playing together. When Angela asked for examples, Elijah's mother said, "The last time Joshua was over, they were playing with Legos, and Joshua was so obsessed with getting everything exactly right and squared off, that they couldn't really play. When Elijah told Joshua that he didn't care if all of the colors matched, Joshua became very agitated and began throwing the blocks around. One of them hit our dog in the eye, hurting her badly enough that we had to take her to the vet. That really upset Elijah."

Later that night, Angela told her husband about the conversation. They were both concerned with the burst of frustration that had resulted in the harm to Elijah's dog, and agreed that Joshua's perfectionism had crossed a line; it was now making it hard for him to maintain relationships. When perfectionism has a significant impact on the ability to keep friends, or is impairing in some other way, it is time to seek help.

Joshua's experience is not rare, and his story highlights the challenge in knowing when to intervene in a child's perfectionistic tendencies. It's often a struggle to tell when behavior is just normal childhood development (throwing things in frustration is typical for most children at some point) and when it shifts into something that needs intervention. When Joshua's parents realized that it was having a significant impact on his ability to keep friends, even those he cared about very much, they knew the time was right for intervention.

While a certain level of perfectionism can be beneficial (it can help you be diligent about taking needed medication, for example), it can have negative consequences as well. Some tasks must be executed perfectly. I have a friend who piloted the Space Shuttle, docking it with the International Space Station, and of course he had to do it perfectly. There was literally no margin for error. When a job or task demands perfection, negative consequences are far less likely. Negative side effects of seeking perfection come when we seek it in inappropriate venues and activities.

Negative Thinking

The difference between people who have high standards and those who have perfectionism is often not how they deal with catastrophic events, but rather how they handle day-to-day stresses.[5] Because of this, one of the common consequences of perfectionism, negative thinking, can be particularly damaging. Negative self-talk is the voice inside one's head that says, "I'm never going to be good enough" or "Everybody is always better than I am." Negative thinking is the part of perfectionism that brushes up against Impostor Syndrome, and it can have the same results.

Negative thinking and distressing self-talk are key components of low self-esteem, which can lead youth to seek approval in unhealthy ways, including damaging relationships. While we may not look at a teenage girl who is dating a boy who treats her badly and think, "Oh, that's because she's a perfectionist," teasing out the roots of why she chose that particular person might lead us to perfectionism's door.

One element at play here is the natural intensity that often accompanies giftedness.[6] I'm not only referring to the idea of overexcitabilities,[7] which characterize so many gifted persons. It is even more fundamental than that. I was introduced to it when I was living in Europe and learning German. In the German language, especially colloquially, there are several prefixes that act as intensifiers. For example, the word *"der Riese"* means "giant," and you will often see it used as a prefix in front of other words like *"der Fehler"* ("mistake"), to form the word, *"der Riesefehler"* meaning "giant mistake." Among gifted children and adults, we have this same phenomenon, but not with language. It's with emotions and qualities. Virtually everything can be more intense—technicolor as opposed to pastels—and the brighter the person, the greater the intensity and sensitivity. This dynamic can easily lead to catastrophizing of even seemingly insignificant negative experiences or issues. Where a typical child may feel sadness, a gifted child may feel *Riesesadness*. What to one child may simply be a bump in the road, to an intense gifted child it may be Mount Everest. In this dynamic lies one of the keys to understanding perfectionism in gifted children.

Stress

Perfectionism creates a tremendous amount of stress because it is discouraging and exhausting to constantly be seeking something you can't find. Even among mental health professionals, perfectionism is associated with stress and burnout in their profession, something they have labeled "compassion fatigue." If even those with years of training and experience find perfectionism to be stress inducing, it shouldn't surprise us that youth often do as well.

Ten-year-old Samuel found his family's move extremely stressful, as he struggled to make friends and adjust to a new and different school curriculum. He had always bitten his nails and cuticles when under stress, and the move made the habit much worse than it had ever been. When his nail-biting habit became severe enough to require medical treatment, including antibiotics, his parents sought help. The social worker at the children's hospital told Samuel's parents that Samuel said, "I just don't think I can ever get it exactly right at my new school." Because he felt this way, he was never satisfied and even high achievement gave him little or no pleasure.

In some ways, negative thinking is similar to the dream many of us have had where we are trying to run from something that is chasing us, but cannot get away. We can't be perfect, yet we try anyway. Of course, we fail. We try again to be perfect, and we fail again. That causes tremendous stress as we feel a constant cloud of failure hanging over our heads, unable to see or accept that it is not failure to not achieve the unachievable. Samuel was correct; he would never get it exactly right. What counseling helped him realize was that it was not a catastrophe, and in fact it was fine to *not* always be perfect.

Workaholism

Perfectionism can create workaholism. Workaholics subconsciously think, "I can't do anything but do this work because I'm trying so hard to be perfect at it." Sometimes this is hard to assess correctly because many gifted youths have strong task commitment, which looks like workaholism if we're not familiar with the differences. The youth with exceptional task commitment can focus on tasks longer than their typical-learner peers, so they can seem perfectionistic to the untrained eye. When task commitment becomes involuntary—meaning that the child or adult cannot disengage from the work without emotional distress—it shifts to workaholism. While we associate workaholism with adults, perfectionistic youth will sometimes forego family vacations or even dinnertime in favor of homework assignments, believing that good grades are the trump card, no matter what game is being played.

Decreased Social Acceptance

Dan Peters, Executive Director of the Summit Center in California, asserts that gifted youth get along as well or better than their age-group peers with the elderly, the differently abled, the very young, and adults. Unfortunately, their social skills are often judged based on their ability to build and maintain relationships with their chronological-age peers because of our school system's age-based stratification. For gifted youth who struggle to build relationships with age-group peers, perfectionism can be the kiss of death. Remember Joshua and his Legos? In his case, perfectionism can cause decreased social acceptance; other people don't enjoy being around the perfectionistic child or are disinterested in dealing with the frustrating effects of it.

As classrooms increasingly emphasize collaboration, decreased social acceptance affects schoolwork. In a collaborative learning situation, a child with perfectionistic tendencies can take over group assignments if the teacher does not carefully delineate roles and separate responsibility for the grades. Sometimes we will see this on report cards, with phrases like, "has overly high expectations of self and others," communicating to parents that there is an issue.

When perfectionists judge their friends by the same standard with which they are judging themselves, perfectionism affects relationship building. This is not just a youth phenomenon, is it? We all know people who, when we go to their houses we feel intimidated because the house is always perfect. You know the type; the house looks like a museum exhibit of the perfect modern family, as if Pinterest suddenly sprang to life. This situation can decrease your interest in a budding relationship because you don't want them to come to your house where people actually *live*, where there might be a book lying open on the coffee table or a dirty dish on the kitchen counter. Comparisons like this can be particularly hard for children since, as adults, we often have more effective self-talk to manage these feelings of being "less than perfect" than do youth. We realize that we often compare our *everyday* to others' *best*, but children are less able to do that, and may feel intimidated or uncomfortable with friends who insist on everything being perfect.

Risk Avoidance

Of all of the negative consequences of perfectionism, risk avoidance has the greatest impact on growth, both cognitively and in other areas. If youth don't take risks, they will not grow intellectually, and if their abilities are already high, there is often a social risk associated with cognitive risk. One high school student, Joaquin, had a tremendous ability in science to see beyond the lesson and understand how the topic fit in the larger picture. Because of this ability to see both the forest and the trees, his work was often significantly different from that of his peers. In his highly competitive high school, however, this was social suicide. The more his work stood out, the more socially isolated he became from many others who were envious of or threatened by his abilities.

Eventually, realizing he could be either popular or smart, but not both, he persuaded his parents to allow him to leave high school and enroll early in college where large class sizes guaranteed anonymity in his ability. He felt safely hidden in the crowd and in an environment where he could raise questions in class without feeling ostracized.

While early college entrance is a great option for many youth, in Joaquin's case it wasn't necessarily the best choice, although it may have felt like it at the time. The reason it may not have been the best choice is because it came from a reaction rather than a proactive choice and set him up for future disengagement from peers at school and work. Rather than finding a way to be himself within the social construct of school, he abandoned the school. While this works sometimes, it's not always possible, and if it's your only strategy, it can be problematic.

Adults sometimes forget how important the social environment is to school-age youth. Joaquin, together with his parents and teachers, could have considered options such as finding another like-minded student (or a core group of them) with whom to connect. Teachers can be exceptionally helpful in this regard, as they know the students from multiple class periods and see them interacting with peers. Another option would have been to have Joaquin engage in an independent study course guided by the teacher or another mentor, allowing him to explore his interest more privately. Joaquin could also have decided to participate more fully in other social aspects of school that interested him, such as athletics, the arts, or social organizations, to build relationships where people would see him as more than just his brain. Yet another choice would be finding another high school, though it is likely that attention would still need to be given to developing social skills.

Risk avoidance can lead to underperformance, and not just to avoid social awkwardness. It is one of the reasons perfectionism is often associated with what is commonly known as underachievement. If a gifted student avoids taking cognitive risk, she will not achieve at the level her ability would make possible. Because this can have collateral consequences, adults may need to help navigate the path. It is not fair or effective to expect youth to take cognitive risk, but then not help them mitigate the effects of that risk-taking, particularly when the risks are social.

Lack of Motivation

Low motivation can look like risk avoidance, yet it is essentially a separate consequence of perfectionism. Understandably, it is difficult to stay motivated when you are constantly thwarted in your pursuit of the thing you are seeking. Ironically, the students most determined to do incredibly well in school can appear lazy if their desire to be the best leads to a discouragement so deep that it robs them of their motivation to try at all. We've all felt that way when we break a diet or a budget. Instead of correcting our course, sometimes we just throw in the towel and give up altogether, eating not just one donut, but a half-dozen. Of course, not all low motivation is rooted in perfectionism, and it is important to determine other factors at play.

Anxiety

It probably comes as no surprise that anxiety levels are usually higher in persons who are struggling with perfectionistic tendencies. If I feel a strong pressure to avoid making a mistake or doing something less than perfectly, I am likely to have higher than typical levels of anxiety. Underlying this anxiety is because I am attempting the unattainable (i.e., perfection), whether I am the one putting pressure on myself or whether it is pressure from others. Perfectionism can be self-imposed (sometimes called "self-oriented perfectionism" or SOP[8]), as well as coming from outside pressures. In addition to anxiety, it is correlated with depression, anxiety, and anorexia. This is more likely when the person has unusually or unreasonably high standards in a wide variety of areas. In their book *When Perfect Isn't Good Enough: Strategies for Coping with Perfectionism*, Antony and Swinson explain, "the main point to consider here is that the more inflexible your beliefs are and the more situations in which you have inflexible opinions, the more likely you are to run into problems."[9]

The Silver Lining

This discussion of negative consequences of perfectionism can feel discouraging, but not all of the consequences of perfectionism are undesirable. It is important to look at the whole picture when determining the impact on the child. Despite some dispute in the literature on perfectionism, many researchers believe that setting high standards is different from perfectionism, and perfectionism isn't always detrimental.[10]

Perfectionism is sometimes divided into two types—"adaptive" or "maladaptive"—with the difference lying in the perfectionist's coping strategies. Very high standards can be healthy, especially for high ability people. Maladaptive perfectionism is similar to malware in a computer—it hijacks what would be an otherwise useful program and ruins it.

Simply perceiving perfectionism as positive is dangerous, however. It is healthier to reframe the idea of adaptive perfectionism as the seeking of high standards, which is very different. In *Overcoming perfectionism: Finding the key to balance and self-acceptance,* author Ann Smith describes the shift from adaptive to maladaptive perfections, saying, "The desire to be superhuman becomes a problem when we begin to believe that perfection is actually possible and even necessary for self-esteem, success, peace of mind, and acceptance by others. We forget that we have a choice and that we will never reach the goal of perfection. It is at this point that the striving evolves into a compulsion."[11] The question then becomes is this perfectionism or high standards? How can we tell the difference? Here are some questions to help discover whether a child's standards are too high and are causing distress and dysfunction, or whether they are a good match for that child.

Is the Child in *Flow*?

First, is the child deriving pleasure and satisfaction from working hard? This is an important question because many people who are bright and talented enjoy working hard, and the things that other people find relaxing may not be relaxing for the gifted child or adult., In his book *Flow: The Psychology of Optimal Experience,*[12] Csikszentmihalyi describes the state of flow as being when work becomes enjoyable in an intense way such that a person often loses awareness of their surroundings. Many gifted individuals are familiar with this state. They feel an intense and focused concentration during which they feel a sense of personal control over the task. The work itself is rewarding, and the sense of the passage of time is altered such that time seems to go much more quickly than linear time. The person has what is called an "autotelic" experience—an experience that is intrinsically rewarding.

Aaliyah's grandmother took care of her when she was a toddler and before she started school, and noticed that Aaliyah often played with her toys in a way that looked like work because of its intensity. She told her son, Aaliyah's dad, that Aaliyah would often be so focused on her play that she wouldn't notice that it was time to eat. At first, Aaliyah's dad was a little concerned, because it was not typical behavior for a child her age. One evening, he interrupted her while she was building a Lincoln Log structure she'd been working on for three hours, and asked her, "Aaliyah, you've been playing with that a long time. Would you like to do something else?" She looked up at him and said, "Dad! It's only been, like, ten minutes!"

With obvious pride, she proceeded to explain the structure to her dad. Later, he said, "Her whole body radiated happiness; her eyes were shining, and she was bouncing up and down with excitement as she explained it. I realized she had the same sense of satisfaction from that as I had at work when I was fully engaged in a project. Time gets away from me, and it doesn't even feel like work." That's flow.

Many gifted kids and adults find themselves in the state of flow with activities that other people might not find flowy. Their activities are not stressful, but rather more often give them a sense of satisfaction and even comfort. Being busy does not always create tension and worry, even when facing a challenging task. They prefer working or at least being occupied to "relaxing" when relaxing involves doing nothing or very little. So, if the person is deriving enjoyment from the task, even if it appears to be workaholism, it may not feel that way to that person.

Where Are the Standards Coming From?

The second question to ask is, "Are the child's standards based on personal desire or someone else's standards?" What is the child looking for and aiming for? If it is the child's standards, then there is more likelihood that the child can adjust the goals, if needed.

When my youngest son went off to college, he decided he was going to get straight A's. A straight 4.0 was his goal. He arrived at college, and the very first day he called me and said, "I'm going to need to adjust my goal." I asked what happened, and he said, "What happened is a little thing called Advanced Philosophical Writing."

He explained, "I found out that at my college an A is a ninety-three or above. If you get a ninety, a ninety-one, or ninety-two, that's an A minus and it only counts as 3.7. So I'm going to let myself be satisfied with either an A or an A minus." That is an example of setting a high goal from personal desire. *He* set the standard; it wasn't that a parent was telling him what he needed to do.

If the high standards are those of the child's, then they are likely to be healthier than if they are set by parents or educators. However, it is important to have laid groundwork for this beforehand. Helping children learn to set reasonable goals when they are young, and allowing them to set their own goals that grow over time, is preventative medicine that can ward off perfectionism later in life. Of course, as every parent knows, children come with personality software preinstalled, and while prevention is wonderful, children with a natural inclination towards perfectionism may not respond in the same way as other children without that inclination, or even at all.

In their book, *When Gifted Kids Don't Have All the Answers*, Judy Galbraith and Jim Delisle explain the proneness of gifted people to perfectionism. They write, "This may be rooted in the awareness of quality. They know the difference between the mediocre and the superior. Once they see how something "ought to be done" (ought to sound, ought to look), they may naturally want to do it that way."[13] Because of this tendency, even those people who are judging themselves by their own standards may set those standards too high. This makes the process of appropriate standard-setting a critical skill for gifted individuals.

Can the Child Relax?

The next question to ask is, "Is the child capable of relaxing?" Asking and answering this question determines the difference between task commitment and perfectionism. As mentioned in the discussion about workaholism, sometimes perfectionistic gifted kids don't even want to stop to eat or sleep when they are working on a project. They don't want to go on family vacations because they just want to work. If the child can say, "You know what? I've done this as well as it needs to be done. This was worth an hour of my life, and now I will relax. I've given it an hour of my life. Let's move on," then that's healthy, even if the child is working very hard. However, the concept of "good enough" can be a difficult one for perfectionists to accept, and it will likely take many discussions and much practice before it becomes a comfortable concept for them

Mastery Orientation

Another important question is, "Is the child's work a matter of mastery orientation, or is it grade oriented?" Occasionally, when I was a high school English teacher, students would turn in a big assignment, like an essay or a research project. As they handed it to me. I would ask, "How do you think you did?" It was very disturbing to me when a child would say something like, "You tell me" or "I'll know when I get my grade back," because my feedback as the teacher, as the evaluator, is only part of the story. Students should have had a feeling of satisfaction from the completion project itself and the accompanying skill development.

If youth are constantly seeking approval, continually seeking someone else's opinion about their work, and have very little sense of satisfaction in the work itself, that's not healthy. But if they can turn something in and say, "I don't know what grade I'm going to get, but I learned how to do this, this, and this," or, "It's way better than the one I did last time, and it's better than what I could have done last year," that's a healthy sign. Before students turn in work, both parents and educators can help youth develop mastery orientation by helping the student reflect on skill acquisition and job satisfaction.

The Desired Answer

The correct answer to all of the questions we've just discussed is "Yes." Is the child deriving pleasure from the work? Is the child setting his own standards? Is the child capable of relaxing? Is the child's feeling about the work not simply based on a grade? And the opposite questions will tell us if the perfectionism is unhealthy. Are the child's feelings based on external standards? Is the child incapable of letting go? Is the child motivated by low self-esteem? Is the child unsatisfied even after a high level of effort? If the answer is "yes," there is a problem with perfectionism. The desirable answer to these questions is, "No."

Understanding the negative consequences of perfectionism, as well as helpful questions to separate adaptive from maladaptive perfectionism, allows both parents and educators to be more effective advocates for youth. If intervention in the form of counseling or other help is needed, the parent who can say, "I think this is a problem because of these specific reasons," will lead to more effective intervention.

A well-matched counselor, experienced in perfectionism, can be helpful. In *The Perfection Deception: Why Trying to be Perfect is Sabotaging your Relationships, Making you Sick, and Holding your Happiness Hostage,*[14] Jane Bluestein describes types of therapies counselors might use.

> *[t]herapeutic techniques might include things like exposure therapy (to gradually develop a tolerance for flaws and imperfections), response prevention (to stop engaging in perfectionistic behaviors), communication training (to identify patterns of judging, criticizing, or attempting to control others), examining the evidence (to confirm or disprove perfectionistic beliefs), changing cognitive processes (to alter perceptions, beliefs, or wishes that result in anxiety or depression), bibliotherapy using content and characters in books to facilitate recovery), distress tolerance, emotional regulation, managing self-talk, learning self-acceptance and self-compassion, or learning to identify and set priorities.*

Parents should never hesitate to seek professional help. Being a parent often requires expertise beyond what we possess.

Can You Measure Perfectionism?

The questions above are subjective ones, but nonetheless provide important information. In addition, there are formal tools to analyze and measure perfectionism. Scales developed by psychologists to evaluate perfectionism include the *Revised Almost Perfect Scale*, the *Perfectionistic Self-Presentation Scale* (PSPS) and the *Multidimensional Perfectionism Scale I* (MPS). Mental health professionals sometimes use these scales when they're evaluating a client who is struggling with anxiety or another condition that can be tangled up with perfectionism.

In the DSM-5 (*Diagnostic and Statistical Manual, Fifth Edition*), used by mental health professionals to evaluate and diagnose mental health issues, some diagnoses include perfectionism in their criteria. One of these diagnoses is Obsessive-Compulsive Personality Disorder. It makes sense, doesn't it? Taken to the extreme, perfectionism could become obsessive and debilitating.

Obsessive-Compulsive Personality Disorder is a fairly uncommon diagnosis especially among kids, yet it's worth looking at because it helps us see how, left unaddressed, perfectionism can hinder our children when they grow into adults. Obsessive-Compulsive Personality Disorder is quite different from Obsessive-Compulsive Disorder, even though the names are confusingly similar. According to the DSM-5, Obsessive-Compulsive Personality Disorder is a pervasive pattern of preoccupation with orderliness, perfectionism, and mental and interpersonal control, at the expense of flexibility, openness, and efficiency. For someone to be diagnosed with Obsessive-Compulsive Personality Disorder, a pervasive pattern has to begin by early adulthood, and it has to occur in a variety of contexts. If someone only manifests these symptoms in one setting, such as school, the criteria for diagnosis is not met. In addition to Obsessive-Compulsive Personality Disorder, we sometimes see rigid perfectionism in people diagnosed with Autism Spectrum Disorder, particularly the higher-functioning type previously called Asperger's Syndrome.[15] We have to be careful to avoid labeling children or adults based solely on *our* view of them because our role is almost always limited.

In addition to the description above, the diagnosis criteria specify that there must be significant impairments in personality functioning, means that even if people demonstrate the pervasive patterns, it's not a disorder unless their lives are significantly impaired and they cannot function normally. When we look carefully at the criteria for Obsessive-Compulsive Personality Disorder,[16] the criteria allow us to see when perfectionism slides over to the problematic side of the continuum. Remember, someone has to have multiple instances of these manifestations occurring together, so don't become overly concerned when some of this resonates with you about a child or even yourself. Personality disorders are not commonly diagnosed in children, and we're not trying to diagnose people with Obsessive-Compulsive Personality Disorder by learning about this; in fact, the opposite is true. Rather, we're trying to get a better idea of what perfectionism can look like when it's manageable, versus when it's really out of control.

The impairment aspect is extremely important. One of the criteria in the DSM-5 states that the person has to be preoccupied with details, rules, lists, order, organization, or schedules to the extent that the major point of the activity is lost in a negative way. Additional criteria include "perfectionism that interferes with task completion (e.g., is unable to complete a project because his or her own overly strict standards are not met)," excessive devotion "to work and productivity to the exclusion of leisure activities and friendships" (there is that workaholism we talked about earlier), over-conscientiousness, scrupulousness, and "inflexibility about matters of morality, ethics, or values (not accounted for by cultural or religious identification)." The last two criteria are an inability "to discard worn-out or worthless objects even when they have no sentimental value" and a reluctance "to delegate tasks or to work with others unless they submit to exactly his or her way of doing things."[17]

This may sound like a perfectionist you know; however, it's important to keep in mind this is not an either/or situation. Individuals can manifest these traits and still not have them interfere with their ability to function well in your life. The criteria, though, are helpful to know as we decide whether to intervene and what signs to watch for, and they also give us language with which to discuss behavior in more objective way. It's less confrontational to say to a child, "It seems like you're a little reluctant to delegate tasks to the people in your group at school" than to say, "Your teacher says you're bossy." Again, avoid the temptation towards armchair diagnosis. If you feel that your child does need professional help, find a counselor who has some familiarity with the instruments that exist to help determine where on the perfectionist continuum the child falls. And, be sure to choose a professional experienced in typical behaviors of gifted children, such as intensity, sensitivity, and high ideals.

The Procrastination Habit

Procrastinating is a form of perfectionism, but it is not exactly the same as procrastination as a habit. It's important to separate the two so that we don't think that every child who procrastinates is a perfectionist. I would argue that not all procrastination is bad[18]. For example, many of us have an inbox, either for paper or email, that we allow to grow until we finally take the time to cull through it all. What do we find? Often, we find that things we kept, thinking they would need attention, but are no longer essential and can be discarded. Although we may feel guilty about not keeping ourselves at "inbox zero," it actually saves us time in the long run.

In his book *Wait: The Art and Science of Delay*, Frank Partnoy explains, "active procrastination is smart; it simply means managing delay, putting off projects that really don't need to be done right away."[19] Gifted individuals are prone to this type of procrastination because they often have what entrepreneur Paul Kedrosky describes as, "nagging suspicion that a lot of the things that I get asked to do I don't actually have to do." It doesn't take gifted students many experiences with busy work to decide that they don't find it worth their time. Also, they are excellent at figuring out the percentage of the grade that is calculated from different types of assignments, so they only do the minimum necessary for the desired grade. Procrastination becomes a part of that plan.

There's a difference, too, between people who think that the work they're given, whether it's a school assignment or an email, is unworthy of them and those who think they work better under pressure. Bronson and Merriman, in their book *Top Dog*, describe "warriors" (people with a fast-acting dopamine-clearing enzyme thanks to their COMT genes) and explain how they often perform better under the pressure of high-stress environments than those with a slower acting enzyme.[20] This is different, however, from people who deliberately choose to put off necessary tasks until the last moment. Although many people think they work best under pressure, the research just doesn't bear this out.

So why do people procrastinate even if it's not working for them? We all have a bias toward present reward, and the further off a possible reward is, the less valuable we think it is. This phenomenon is called hyperbolic discounting. Because bright kids love big words and the back-stories, you can share these ideas with even very young children. I call it, "trading what you want most for what you want now." The connection between hyperbolic discounting and procrastination is a way of saying, "What I'm doing now is worth more to me than that assignment due in six weeks." Gifted children are particularly susceptible to this thinking because sometimes they receive very little satisfaction from completing school assignments they perceive as too simple, or are indeed difficult but not complex enough to be interesting. Perfectionists may try to bargain away assignments that are in the future, usually larger projects, turning instead to assignments that are more straightforward and due tomorrow. They know they can do a worksheet with a much greater chance of a perfect score than an essay or project.

The neurochemical dopamine plays a role in this dynamic. Dopamine is the chemical of motivation, giving us a boost and feeling of well-being when we accomplish (or even anticipate accomplishing) a task of value to us. For long projects, we often wait too long between dopamine releases to keep us motivated. Students often get the dopamine-sponsored feeling of satisfaction from small assignments because a little dopamine is released when we finish a task. If you say, "Done!" even more is released! It makes sense, then, that reasonable people might choose to get lots of dopamine by doing small things, even at the expense of possible future dopamine release from a big project due down the road.

Many schools have internet portals for parents where they can check their children's progress and grades. This type of procrastination can be problematic in those situations because the grade in a class may look stable and fine until a big project is due and the student earns a zero. Because these types of projects are often due at the end of a grading period, a parent might check the grade on a Friday and see an A, and then when the report card comes home, the grade has dropped a full letter grade or more. I've done that as a teacher before I realized how problematic it is for parents. I decided to break up big projects into chunks, having semi-formal check-ins for those steps. I assigned grades on those steps so that parents could see those grades and recognize early on if the project isn't progressing appropriately. If a teacher doesn't do this, parents can help their children create a timetable for the project's progression and the child can check off completed steps as the project moves along. This technique also helps infuse some regular dopamine release into long-term projects as the student completes intermediate goals along the way.

Now I am not one to say that all procrastination is bad. Many people work best when they have a little adrenaline flowing with last minute work. It's not really a good idea to tell people, "You'll never do your best work at the last minute," because that's not always true. The difficulty is when people are not adept at finding the balance between the effective last minute and the too-late last minute. So, let's define last minute. In a project that was assigned a week ago, the last minute might be the night before, but when a teacher gives six weeks to do a project, a week before it is due may actually be the last minute. As kids grow and learn how to manage time, it's important to help them learn this executive functioning skill of planning and time-management. They must learn that last minute doesn't necessarily mean the literal last minute, and adults must teach them how.

As it was with Joshua, it is with many youths. If the child is to live an emotionally healthy life, there is a need for change, and the perfectionism must be addressed. While not all people who struggle with perfectionistic tendencies have the same negative effects of that struggle, some social and emotional costs are common among both youth and adults. Because there are few links between perfectionism and actual achievement, parents and educators should not hesitate to intervene if the negative impact of the perfectionism is interfering with the child's cognitive, social, or emotional development or happiness. The same is true for adults; if our own perfectionism is a detriment rather than an asset, we should feel confident that seeking help is warranted and reasonable.

Key Ideas

- Perfectionism has negative consequences, including negative thinking, stress, workaholism, anxiety, decreased social acceptance, a lack of motivation, and risk avoidance.
- Gifted youth often have strong task commitment, which can look like perfectionism.
- When we are working hard at rewarding, appropriately challenging work, we can enter a state of *flow*.
- If perfectionism gets out of hand, it can become pathological and require mental health care.
- There are instruments that measure perfectionism developed and used by mental health professionals.
- Procrastination can be a reasonable reaction to work we deem unworthy of us, and it must be managed to avoid to having a detrimental impact on performance.

Action Steps

- Look through the negative consequences of perfectionism and rate yourself and/or your child on a scale of 1 – 5 (5 being severe) on each consequence.
- Ask the questions posed in the chapter to give yourself a sense of whether you feel that high standards are becoming perfectionistic in a maladaptive way.
- Model for your child or students the concept of good enough, as well as finding satisfaction in mastery and a job well done. Say things like, "I feel really good about this thing I did, even though it didn't come out like the picture. I learned how to do something new, and that feels good."
- Set reasonable standards for yourself, and make those standards known. Often, adults appear to be more masterful to children than children feel they themselves are; this can breed perfectionism
- Help youth set timelines and break down larger tasks into sub-goals, avoiding the negative impact of procrastination.
- Discuss your own tendencies towards procrastination and be honest about when you feel its tug. Help youth understand that while it's tempting to delay working on a task, we know our best results will almost always come when we give ourselves enough time. Use reflection questions like, "What can happen if we wait until the last minute?" or "How well would it work if Dad didn't decide what to make for dinner until 6pm when we have to be at soccer practice at 6:45pm?"

Excellent is Good Enough

When Juan started third grade, his parents noticed an almost immediate change in him. Homework became a daily ordeal. After school, Juan's mother could barely get him in the car before he would be digging through his backpack to start on his homework. He would park himself at the kitchen table and stay there until he was forced to stop for dinner, and then bedtime. He became easily frustrated with his work, often crying or tearing the paper in exasperation. He began to complain of stomach aches, but he didn't want to miss school, even when he was running a fever. He declined to go on field trips, not wanting to miss any school, even when every other student in his grade was going.

Juan's mother, Dulce, requested a conference, but neither she nor the teacher were able to figure out what was really going on. Juan insisted he liked his teacher, and the teacher seemed to genuinely like Juan. The teacher gave Juan frequent positive feedback, and encouraged him with appropriate praise for his effort in class. Dulce finally took Juan to a therapist who specialized in working with gifted children.

After working with Juan for two months, the therapist told Dulce that the shift from ungraded work in second grade to graded work in third grade had awakened a "sleeping perfectionist dragon." Prior to this year, Juan's school had just given pass or fail grades, along with descriptive evaluation. Now that a "100" had become the goal for every assignment, Juan was feeling tremendous pressure to achieve 100 on all of his assignments. This perfectionism was preventing him from participating in many fun and normal activities for kids his age. In time, with the help of the therapist and the cooperation of his teacher and parents, Juan learned how to back away from the need to achieve a perfect score on every assignment.

One of the reasons high-ability people struggle with perfectionism to a greater extent than the general population is simply that they *are* capable of very high performance. This capability can easily morph into a perfectionist compulsion to achieve at the highest levels in every area all of the time. Sometimes schools and families, with the best of intentions, inadvertently contribute to this dynamic with subtle (and sometimes not-so-subtle) pressure to perform. Slogans like "always give your best" are encouraging to some children, but to a perfectionist, they throw down a mentally unhealthy gauntlet.

The Pursuit of Excellence

Of course, it is appropriate for gifted individuals to pursue excellence, but there is a fine line between the pursuit of excellence and disabling perfectionism, and this balance can be tricky to navigate. As discussed in Chapter 2, even researchers disagree about whether perfectionism can be adaptive or not. Because of this, it is important for adults to share the message that excellent effort and learning—not perfect scores or complete mastery—is always good enough. We must not only give lip service to that message, we must believe it and model it. We have to believe and demonstrate that an A- is truly is as acceptable to us as an A+. Yet even those of us who believe this and want to share that belief with our children may be challenged by systems that split hairs when it comes to grades, particularly in school environments that are highly competitive.

Miriam Adderholdt includes a helpful pursuit of excellence versus perfectionism chart in her book *Perfectionism: What's bad about being too good?*[21]

The Pursuit of Excellence	Perfectionism
Doing the research necessary for a term paper, working hard on it, turning it in on time, and feeling good about what learned.	Doing three drafts, staying up two nights in a row, and handing your paper in late because you had to get it right (and still feeling bad about your paper).
Studying for ka test, taking it with confidence, and feeling good about your score of 96.	Cramming at the last minute, taking the test with sweaty palms, and feeling bad about your 96 because a friend got a 98.
Choosing to work on group projects because you enjoy learning from the varied experiences and approaches of different people.	Always working alone because no one can do as good a job as you, and your are not about to let anyone else slide by on *your* A.
Accepting an award with pride even though the engraver misspelled your name. (You know it can be fixed later.)	Accepting the award resentfully because those idiots did not get your name right.
Reading the story you wrote for the school paper and noticing that the editor improved the copy.	Throwing a fit because the editor tampered with your work.
Going out with people who are interesting, likable, and fun to be with.	Refusing to go out with people who are not stellar athletes, smart, and popular.

The Pursuit of Excellence	Perfectionism
Being willing to try new things, take risks, and learn from your experiences and your mistakes.	Avoiding new experiences because you are terrified of making mistakes, especially in public.
Deciding to babysit to earn some extra money, taking a babysitting class through the local park district.	Deciding to organized and run a babysitting service for all of the families from the local elementary school.
Keeping your room cleaner and neater, making your bed more often, and putting your clothes away.	Not being able to leave the room until the bed and room are just so.
Taking tennis lessons and playing two or three times a week to have fun and joining a competitive league to challenge yourself.	Taking lessons as often as you can, practicing every day, and not feeling satisfied until you can beat every other player in your league.

Because the book is geared to teens, the chart is as well. Yet it's an easy transfer for parents of younger kids to see how situations they could find themselves in could be considered in similar ways.

Sometimes our environments create a situation that almost forces kids into seeking perfection. In Texas, for example, if you are in the top 10% of your graduating class, you are guaranteed admission to most state universities. This creates an extremely competitive environment, with many school districts calculating GPA on a 12-point scale, as opposed to the more common 4-point scale. On a 12-point scale, students can be separated in rank by a thousandth of a point. This encourages students to play the GPA Game, a dynamic in which students take certain classes but avoid others, not because of anything to do with learning, but rather because of their effect on one's GPA. Students who have been enjoying orchestra class for years will drop it because it doesn't have an honors boost for the GPA. Students take classes online in order to avoid required classes that don't come with an honors option. It's a system that encourages cheating along with perfectionism.[22]

Unfortunately, parents and teachers have little power to change entire systems. In these environments, it becomes even more important for the parents and educators around the students to avoid creating a culture of perfectionism where an A+ is the only thing that's acceptable. The way to do this is to look at the different situations that contribute to the creation of the environment.

Parent Reactions and Setting Goals

Consider how we react when a child comes home with a report card. Sometimes it's as if the lowest grade is printed in a different color ink from the rest of the grades. We'll look at the report card and say something like, "Wow, great job in biology and all of these other classes, but what's the deal with this ninety in English?" Too often, we focus on the lowest grade, even if it's not that low, and we focus our action on that. We emphatically ask, "What can you do to bring that grade up?"

Instead of looking at just the grades, consider asking questions such as, "How much did you learn in these classes this semester?" or "Do you feel that these grades reflect your effort?" Other helpful questions include, "Do you feel like your plan for this class is working?" or "What do you think had the biggest impact on this grade?" Questions like this are much healthier and far less likely to create a climate of perfectionism than those like, "Can you bring that grade up to match your other grades?"

Goal setting with perfectionists works best if the student sets his or her own objectives and revisits them reflectively as the grading period goes on. The old saying, "Good, better, best/ never let it rest/ until the good is better/ and the better is best" is a recipe for disastrous perfectionism. We should not demand that youth constantly strive to improve even very high grades or performances. At some point, what they are doing must be good enough. If not, they will never be able to move forward in areas of interest, as they are forced to allocate limited resources of time and attention to everything they do as they attempt to improve in every possible domain.

Creating Climates of Perfectionism

The need for adjustment of expectations is true of teachers as well as parents. Often, we focus only on bringing grades up, rather on the other components of scholarship and successful school experience. Educators should step back from the practice of only rewarding perfect scores. Don't reserve all of your scratch-and-sniff stickers for the 100's. We can put stickers and happy faces on papers that students have done that show effort, not just perfection. If we only reward perfect, we are creating a climate in which perfectionism flourishes. The perfect medium for the growth of perfectionism is the practice of only rewarding perfect work. In addition to stickers and happy faces, we should consider the work we're displaying as exemplary work we want other students to model after. Can we consider adding in work that shows gain? That shows effort? By doing this, we send the message that we notice progress, not just perfect.

Many of us have heard the saying, "Anything worth doing is worth doing well." I don't agree with that. A corollary of that might be, "Anything not worth doing is not worth doing well." I believe that anything worth doing is worth doing as well as it needs to be done. Consider taking out the trash. We can probably all agree that it's an activity worth doing. However, what does it mean to do it well? Should we tie the little red plastic tie in a perfect bow? Should we pull out a protractor and line the trash can up perfectly perpendicular to the curb? Should we sterilize the can every day or line it with essential oils? This may seem like an exaggeration, yet people often feel pressured to work very hard on things that mean very little—and sometimes we pressure our children in similar fashion. Searching for excellence, or even "good enough," as opposed to perfection means giving the most to the things that matter most.

The Level Strategy

An effective strategy for teaching the idea that perfect isn't always necessary is to assign activities a level on a scale of one to five, with one being low effort and five being top effort.

This works for school assignments, as well as household chores. Activities that are **Level One** are things that just need to be done, but don't necessarily need to be done well. These are things that need what my grandmother would call "giving it a lick and a promise." For example, I have three sons, so there are a lot of beds in my house, and I like those beds made. Making them is a Level One. I don't need the little pillows perfectly arranged or the throw artfully arranged across the foot of the bed. I don't need the opening of the pillowcase facing away from the door like I used to have to do when I was a volunteer at a hospital as a teenager. I don't expect these beds to be featured in a picture on Pinterest. I just want the beds made. I want the duvet pulled up and the pillows off the floor. That's a Level One.

A **Level Two** is something that is worth doing a little better than a Level One. Level Two activities may require additional attention or have more criteria for acceptable work. There may be a slightly higher skill or level of care required to do the task satisfactorily. To continue the household analogy, this would be something like cleaning the toilet. It should be done to a certain standard, but there is more than one right way to do it, and it doesn't need to take a large investment of time. This example underscores how sometimes a task can shift levels, depending upon the circumstance. The toilet must be cleaned reasonably well, and sometimes a sanitizing wipe is enough. However, there will be other times (e.g., company is coming, there have been a lot of guests, someone has been ill, etc.) where it requires a lot more attention. In a school environment, a Level Two could be math practice worksheets. They need to be done to master the material, and they take some skill to do, but you don't typically need all of your ability or large quantities of time to complete them, nor does the appearance of the paper need to be immaculate.

A **Level Three** requires a higher level of effort. It takes more than a few minutes to complete, demands some focused concentration, and/or takes some practice to get it right. In a school, this would be the typical in-class assignment or homework assignment that is a single, discrete task. It is likely worth more time than a Level Two, and if it's not done well, there might be significant natural negative consequences. At home, a Level Three would be washing the dishes. If it's not done well, disease and sickness can result, and it may take some practice to get it right.

Level Four tasks require more time, effort, or skills than Level Three activities. At school, bigger projects that extend over a period of time would be Level Fours, not just because they take more time, but also because they likely are more complex and count for more than, say, a regular homework assignment. Failing to do them can create severe consequences. Tasks that take extensive preparation will also be Level Four tasks. Level Four is the highest task that a school assignment can be.

A **Level Five** is a task or activity in which something critically important is at stake. When I severed a tendon in my foot and the surgeon was operating on it, his work was a Level Five. A mistake could have left me unable to walk for the rest of my life. Level Five activities may be things like taking a test that determines if you get into the college of your dreams, making sure medication is taken as directed, or attending a relative's wedding. Level Fives are worth Level Five effort. They are worth time.

They are worth a plan. They are worth a little worry. Note however, that there are essentially no typical school assignments that require Level Five effort, precision, and care.

The difficulty is that perfectionists act as if *everything* is a Level Five, when in reality most things are a Level Three. As teachers and parents, we can label the level of the work to be done as a way to build communication and to help children avoid over-valuing minor tasks. When I'm giving an assignment to students, I actually write in the upper right-hand corner of the page what level it is. A normal homework assignment would either be a Level Two or a Level Three. I also include how much time I think it should take, so it would look like this "3/20"—indicating a Level Three activity worth twenty minutes of time. This also helps parents understand what's expected when they're working with a child on homework. If, as a parent, I see that the teacher thinks the assignment should take twenty minutes, I know it's a problem if my child is sitting there for an hour and a half.

Another benefit of this strategy is that it improves home-school communication. Conflict can arise between home and school when a child brings home assignments that she is spending three hours on, and the parent is frustrated, thinking, "My daughter is only seven!" The teacher is totally unaware of the parent's frustration because the teacher felt that the assignment was only a ten- or fifteen-minute project. The teacher has no way of knowing that the child, perhaps from perfectionistic tendencies, is dragging the work out or unnecessarily worried about a relatively unimportant assignment. The simple act of identifying the level along with the amount of time can be helpful in improving the home-school connection and developing mutual understanding.

If your child is really struggling with perfectionism or its accompanying anxiety, it might be worthwhile to make an agreement that the child will only be expected to work on the assignment for the amount of time the teacher feels the work is worth and will grade only that work. Eventually, as the child grows in confidence and anxiety diminishes, she will get more done in that time. Some teachers may struggle with this, thinking, "How can I grade that child based on a small amount of work when everybody else did the whole assignment?" I would argue that that is part of differentiating instruction. We need to differentiate in the affective domain as well. Educators are often required to adjust assignments for students with learning disabilities, yet we don't need a federal law to force us into doing what's best for children.

The Timing Strategy

A corollary to this strategy is that if there is a task that a child (or even adult!) resists, the task can be timed. When we are under time pressure, we often find that the task we hated and put off doing really only takes a few minutes to complete. We may have been spending more effort and mental energy in avoiding the task than we would have in completing it. My least favorite chore for years was changing sheets. With four beds in the house to be changed, it just felt like a daunting challenge. I would put it off or make bargains with myself about doing it. Because my children all have allergies, washing their sheets in hot water every week was an important Level Four chore. I finally took my own advice and timed it. It took me all of seven minutes to change a king-sized bed. Seven minutes! That was clearly not worth the angst I had been inflicting on myself.

We also use this strategy when working together as a family on tasks. By setting a timer, we can see if we can get the chores completed at the appropriate level in a certain amount of time. All of my sons can give you a pretty close guess as to how long it will take us to clean up the entire house after we've had a big party because we've timed it repeatedly. You can make it even more fun by creating a playlist of songs that equal the amount of time the task takes, and then play that list as you complete the task. For instance, if cleaning out the backpack after school is an issue, time it. Then search for a song that lasts a matching length of time. As the backpack is organized at the end of the day, play the song. If you can get faster at the task while maintaining the right level of quality, pick shorter songs. This makes it feel more like a game than a chore.

Part of the time-setting strategy includes setting the "go over" time limit. Usually, I'd suggest ten percent. For example, it's fine to go a minute over something you think should take ten minutes, but not five minutes over. If it's the first time you've completed a task, it may be hard to guess how long it will take, so you may need to be flexible the first couple of times a task is done. A "go over" time limit can help mitigate perfectionism. If something is taking much longer than it should, stop, take a break, and return to it.

One thing to keep in mind is that levels can shift. If my mother-in-law is coming to visit, the chores that last week were a Level One may shift to a Level Five (Is there a Level Six?) for the duration of her visit. Or it may be worth the extra effort to make the beds perfectly if the house is for sale and we're impressing buyers. The same math facts practice that is typically a Level Two turns into a Level Four if it's a final assessment that determines how much work is needed for mastery or grade level promotion.

Parents and educators can list common activities and assignments, and then carefully consider with which level the activity or assignment is aligned. Talking with children about what the different levels look like at home and school provides a common vocabulary for discussion. It's less confrontational to say, "Hmm, I was thinking that cleaning your room was a Level Three activity, and you spent ten minutes doing it. What level do you think it is? Do you think ten minutes was about the right amount of time for that level?"

The Importance of Reflection

A key part of all of these strategies is reflection because such thinking helps us to shape our self-talk and our expectancies. Remember, it seldom is the task that causes us anxiety; rather, it is what we say to ourselves about the task—our self-talk. After a task is completed or some activity comes to an end, spend some time reflecting on how it went from the perspective of appropriate standards. This doesn't need to be formal; it can be a car conversation. The key is to provide an opportunity for the child to look back on the completed activity and decide if the level chosen was accurate, if the time spent was on target, and if the standard set (the grade, for example) was appropriate.

Jeremiah's teachers noticed he was showing perfectionistic behavior at school. Working with his parents, they began using the level and timing strategies, along with having him set his own goals for performance. After a task was completed, either his dad (with whom he lived) or a teacher would spend a few minutes debriefing him and guiding his thinking by gently asking questions. While they were on their way to soccer practice or other activities, Jeremiah's dad would ask questions such as, "So, you set a goal to get a 92 on that project. What do you think about that goal now that you got it back?" or "Was Level Four too high for that poster or was it just about right?" As he gained confidence in his ability to set his own goals and to be realistic about how much effort particular tasks were worth, both Jeremiah's teachers and his dad both noticed a decrease in his anxiety, as well as his increased use of "Levels" at school. His math teacher called his dad after school to say that she had overheard Jeremiah, who is ten, saying to another student, "Look, is it possible you're treating this like a Level Four, when it's really only a Level Two?"

Some people do best with private reflection, and a journal can serve as a good way for them to reflect. It's important not to over-track, as that can increase perfectionistic behavior, so this doesn't mean recording scores or weight or distance or time. It means looking at the standards that were set and reflecting on their appropriateness. Adults should model these behaviors by making their own reflection visible to youth by talking out loud. When I was teaching, I would reflect on lesson plans with my students, inviting them into my thought processes. I might say something like, "I had set a goal for 90% student engagement in that activity, but I think that was too low. I ended up with higher engagement, so next time I may set my goal higher."

In our own reflection, we need to remember that sometimes perfectionism gets cultivated and nurtured by environments that nurture perfectionism. Although parents and educators don't have full control over all aspects of the systems in place that can add to perfectionism, strategies such as the ones described above can decrease the likelihood that those systems will have a negative impact on students. The adults in a child's life have a greater impact than they know, and these straightforward strategies can be very helpful in helping students avoid the painful consequences of system-based perfectionism.

Key Ideas

- Pursuing excellence is different from perfectionism, and is appropriate for high-ability individuals.
- Adults should avoid developing climates and habits of perfectionism.
- Youth can be taught to set their own goals, rather than having performance goals imposed upon them.
- Strategies such as identifying levels and setting time limits can help to curb perfectionistic behavior.
- Reflection time after a task is completed is essential.

Action Steps:

- Evaluate the system-based perfectionism in your environment. Just naming it makes you feel more in control of it and can lead to powerful discussions about how to manage it.
- Discuss the idea of levels, using the chart below, and determine the level that matches the task. Let children provide examples.
- Commit to stop an activity within the 10% overtime limit. If the task must be completed and is not done, then take a break and do something else for an equal amount of time before resuming.
- List a few common chores or activities and time how long it takes to do them. Record the times. Try to beat the times while keeping the level the same (don't sacrifice necessary quality for the sake of beating the record).
- Match tasks to a song or playlist of songs. If the task is a verbal task like homework that must be read or math problems, select music without words.
- Build reflection time into family conversations or get a journal to record private reflection.

TASK	LEVEL I'VE BEEN ACTING AS IF IT IS	LEVEL MOST PEOPLE WOULD AGREE IT IS	HOW I SHOULD ADJUST MY BEHAVIOR (IF NEEDED)
		63	

Goals, the Journey, and Everything In Between

As you set out for Ithaka, hope the voyage is a long one, full of adventure, full of discovery.

\- CONSTANTINE KAVAFY

In the Ionian Sea to the west of continental Greece lies the fabled island of Ithaka. It is the second smallest of the seven main Ionian Islands, yet its story looms large in our exploration of perfectionism. Ithaka is best known from Homer's epic poem *The Odyssey*. After Homer tells the story of the Trojan War in *The Iliad*, he brings Odysseus home in *The Odyssey*, a journey that takes longer than the war itself took to fight. Odysseus has angered Poseidon, the god of the sea, by blinding his son, Polyphemus, and in punishment, Poseidon makes Odysseus's journey as long as possible. Along the way, Odysseus and his men encounter a wide variety of monsters and challenges. They encounter the angry Cyclops who eats six of the men before Odysseus is able to escape. They get caught between the six-headed monster Scylla and the violent whirlpool Charybdis. Circe threatens to turn his men into pigs. Some of his men eat the cattle of the sun god, Helios, and Helios is vastly unpleased.

Some of the challenges they face are goal distractors. They encounter the Lotus Eaters and nearly lose sight of their ultimate purpose. Odysseus is held captive by Calypso on her island Ogygia, as her love slave for eight years (My teenage students never understood why this was a problem.) They pass the Sirens who attempt to lure Odysseus back to his past, and Odysseus has his men tie him to the mast so he won't follow the Sirens, while still being able to listen to them. As they near the island, they are shipwrecked and all of the men are killed except Odysseus who washes ashore, nearly dead himself.

Odysseus has held the dream of Ithaka in his mind while away all of those long years, yet the reality is nothing like what he envisioned. He longs to be reunited with his wife Penelope and see his only child, Telemachus. He wants to resume control of his island kingdom. Exhausted beyond words from his journey, he longs to have life return to pre-war days. So, what happens to Odysseus? He left Ithaka as its king, and now he returns disguised as a beggar. He gets to the island to find that his faithful dog, Argos has been thrown away as trash. His wife Penelope is caught up in a bizarre Greek version of *Bachelorette* where 108 men called *suitors* are vying for her favors. They're trying to get her to marry them so they can become the King. Penelope, desperate to avoid that, weaves a shroud by day, and then unravels it at night, saying she will choose among the suitors when it's finished. When Odysseus arrives, she does not even recognize him.

This was not the utopia about which Odysseus had dreamed. In fact, it was nothing like it at all. The Greek poet, Constantine Cavafy, wrote, "As you set out for Ithaka/ hope the voyage is a long one/ full of adventure, full of discovery." He goes through all the things you may encounter on your journey to Ithaka, and towards the end of the poem says. "And if you find her poor/ Ithaka won't have fooled you/ Wise as you will have become/ you will know what all these Ithakas mean."

The poem ends with the key idea—a truth Cavafy explains, not only of the journey of Odysseus, but of us all when he says. "Ithaka gave you the marvelous journey/ Without her you would not have set out/ She has nothing left to give you now."[23]

The Importance of the Journey

We've all had goals like Ithaka. We think, "Once I get here I'll be happy. Once I get there I'll be content. Once I get into high school, once I turned fifteen, once I can drive, once I can go to college, once I get the job I want, once I get the spouse I want, once I have a house, once I have children, once the kids are grown." This kind of thinking creates an unhealthy, unachievable, and self-defeating view of the purpose of our goals.

It is vitally important to keep in mind the message Kavafy shares with us: it's not about finally getting there. It's about the journey, and it always was. Goals exist to give us the journey. The goal of going to college exists to give us a productive, invaluable learning experiences before we get there. The goal of becoming a computer programmer gives us the incentive to work away on code even though that task isn't always that exciting. The goal to become a ballerina offers the journey of taking classes, developing self-discipline, and an appreciation of the arts that we can apply in all areas of our lives. The goal of cleaning a house is at least partly to provide an appreciation for being lucky to have something of your own to take care of. It's the journey and always was.

Goal Setting

As we are setting goals, we have to be careful not to focus only on the goal, but to consider what journey the goal offers. If we believe the result of the goal will be satisfying, but getting there will be almost unbearable, we need to evaluate whether the goal is truly a good fit. Sometimes it will be, and sometimes it will not. It is important to do a cost-benefit analysis for yourself.

For example, several times in my life I have needed to set fitness goals. I knew I would enjoy achieving the goal. It feels terrific to be in good physical shape. However, getting there is not always pleasant. I live in Texas, and giving up Blue Bell ice cream is not something we take lightly in the Lone Star State. I decided the end result would be worth it.

Other times, this has not been the case. I was accepted into a Ph.D. program in Modern European History, a true passion of mine. I knew I would love earning my doctorate in that subject. However, I had just finished years of graduate school, during which I always felt guilt-ridden, like I was being chased every time I started to read anything without footnotes; I felt like I was cheating or doing something wrong. In spite of how much I knew I would love walking the stage after earning that degree, the journey was going to be too brutal to make it an appropriate goal, and so I began to look for alternate goals.

This is not to say journeys always have to be fun, exciting, or easy; they just need to be worth it in a way that makes sense to you. You have to weigh how much the achievement of the goal will benefit you compared to the opportunity cost of the journey. The journey of Odysseus was worth it because his entire future depended upon his safe arrival back home. The cost of the opportunity was the years of his life he would never get back, but that was outweighed by the end result. His life would have been nearly worthless to him were he not returned home to his family and his island; his entire reason for being was centered there. Sometimes however, like Odysseus, we cannot really know the value of the opportunity until the end of the journey. We can only make our best guess about whether it will be worth the struggle. And during the journey, we must remember to be gentle with ourselves when things do not always go as planned.

For those with high abilities, there are many options of different journeys, opportunities, and possibilities. But these create quandaries and conversations precisely because there are so many possibilities. If I choose the goal of becoming a doctor, I may have to give up another goal that I want as well. My abilities mean that I can be successful in many endeavors, but deciding between the choices can be very difficult. I may feel that *if I can* achieve certain goals, *then I should.*

Perfectionism exacerbates this because it can make us feel that we not only should accept too many goals, but we should also accomplish them with extraordinary proficiency. It can be hard to accept that it is okay to let a goal, even an achievable one, go. Sometimes parents, teachers, or mentors can help gifted children prioritize goals, seek alternate goals, or even creatively combine goals. If a child wants to be a doctor but also an engineer, there is a possibility of studying bioengineering. A child who is musically talented may decide to keep the music as a hobby while pursuing a higher degree in another field.

The Importance of a Cost-Benefit Analysis

Doing a cost-benefit analysis can be more helpful than a simple pro/con list. Pro/con lists do not look carefully enough at the journey, and they often place the goal as a disconnected task, whereas a cost-benefit analysis takes into account that the goal is small part of a larger whole. When Marcos was deciding whether to take AP European History, his teacher guided him through a cost-benefit analysis. Mr. Jameson helped Marcos consider what benefit it would give him, not only at the end of the course in the form of college credit, but also how it would fit into his overall schedule. The cost was not only time, but also giving up another class only available during that same period. In the end, because he had a clear view of its place in the broader scheme of things, Marcos decided not to take the class and had no regrets, even though he imagined it would have been a great experience.

One part of such decisions is to consider what the accomplishment of the goal will allow you to do in the future. Part of why I decided not to pursue the doctorate was because I didn't need a Ph.D. to do what I wanted to do personally or professionally. Had I needed a Ph.D., for instance, if I had a desire to teach at a university, it would have factored into my decision. On the other hand, I've taken courses I knew I wouldn't like because they were prerequisites for courses I wanted or needed to take. Perfectionists sometimes set goals for themselves involving journeys that aggravate the perfectionism, neglecting to consider that the goals do not actually expand their future prospects in any meaningful way.

Ironically, once you have arrived at the goal, the first thing you must do after celebrating is to set a new goal. We can help kids understand it isn't really about the goal itself, but about the journey, and we must set out on a new journey once we reach our goal. Like stones in a stream, goals exist to help us reach closer towards the next goal. They are rarely the ends of the road. The reason this is so important is that people who struggle with perfectionism can be too goal-focused and too little focused on the journey. They expect the goal to make them feel complete, satisfied, worthy, and happy. In doing this, they lose the joy of the journey, consistently finding the meeting of the goal unsatisfying because they were expecting it to do something it could not—and was never meant to—do.

How can you help others to do a cost-benefit analysis? To be effective guides in this process, be careful not to let your own biases and opinions overshadow the child's own intuition and reasoning. If the child makes a decision you do not agree with, and subsequently regrets her decision, she will learn from having practiced the cost-benefit analysis process that you have gently guided her through.

Tiny Habits

A particularly effective way to break perfectionists out of the habit of inappropriate goal-setting is to use the strategy called "Tiny Habits." Developed by behavioral scientist B.J. Fogg,[24] the idea is that your best chance for creating a new behavior is to add a small, discrete habit to a habit that is already established. Fogg's argument is that only three things have the potential to spark real change: an epiphany, an environmental change, or to take baby steps. His Tiny Habits model focuses on the third possibility.

The first step in Fogg's design is to simplify the behavior. Let's say your goal is to learn Latin. The first step would be to say, "I'm going to work with my Latin language program for thirty seconds every day" or "I'm going to practice with 20 flashcards every day." You can see the difference between those manageable goals as compared with a sweeping declaration of "I'm going to master Latin." These small steps should take thirty seconds or less to complete. Examples of small goals might include things like:

- Practice one line in handwriting book
- Pick up two toys
- Brush dog thirty seconds
- Write one sentence in journal
- Recycle one piece of paper
- Read one paragraph of my history book
- Do one math problem
- Address one envelope

Fogg calls these "TSBSMs" – The Smallest Behavior That Matters. One of the reasons this works well for people struggling with perfectionism is that when you break a goal down, you live in the possible and concrete.

Perfectionists often struggle with setting huge, hairy goals for themselves that set them up for failure. Instead of saying, "I want to earn an A on this test," they say (often just to themselves), "I'm never going to get a 'B' in my life." Instead of setting a goal to graduate from college, they set a goal to be the first person to ever graduate in five semesters with a 4.0 with a double major and three minors. This increases the likelihood of perfectionistic defeatism that so often follows. As one colleague said, "Yard by yard is hard, but inch by inch is a cinch."

The second step in Fogg's method is to find a way to place this new habit into your already existing daily habits. This is key; you're finding something that is already in place every single day to which to attach the new, tiny habit. This is the *anchor habit*. If you are already in the habit of eating breakfast, you could do your flashcards right after breakfast. If you already have a time every day where you like to read or watch TV, you could do the cards then. Run through them after you take a shower. Do you see how this works? You essentially hook the new tiny habit onto a bigger, more established habit. You're not leaving the new habit swaying in the breeze on its own, but melding it to an already successful habit. It's best if this habit is one that is done at a typical time each day to make it easier to accomplish.

While you could attach the new habit to the existing habit, either before, during, or after it, Fogg strongly recommends attaching it afterwards. His reasoning is this: when you attach it after the existing habit, the existing, established habit becomes a trigger for the new habit. It becomes its own reminder. If you say, "I'm going to listen to one thirty-second clip of classical music before I get in the car," you will have a lot of mornings where you get in the car, slap your forehead with your palm, and say, "I forgot!" If, however, you say, "I'm going to listen to one thirty-second clip of classical music after I walk the dog," walking the dog becomes a reminder to do the listening. This won't always work or be practical, in which case you can do it *before* or *during* the established habit (study flashcards while you eat breakfast, for example), but try also to find an *after*.

The third and final step in the Tiny Habits model is to do what Fogg calls "train the cycle." You must make this new, small habit as much a part of your routine as the big habit it was attached to. Fogg warns that you will need reminders in the beginning, so don't see the need for reminders as a failure. You are rewiring your brain, and that isn't immediate. One suggestion Fogg shares is to increase the possibility of success is to resist the temptation to grow the habit quickly or to focus on large changes. Keep it small and keep it simple, until it becomes as much a part of your life, as automatic, as the habit to which you attached it. Suggestions for helping to set reminders include:

- Put a sticky note on the shower door with a reminder of what you're supposed to do.
- Store the materials you need next to the materials for the established habit (e.g., put the flashcards next to the medicine cabinet with your toothbrush).
- Use one of the many habit apps for your phone to send you reminders at the right time.
- Attach an index card to the headboard of your bed.

You will miss a few times in the beginning, but that's okay; you're in training. Simply refocus and set a new reminder system. You will do best to change up your reminder system every now and then so that your brain doesn't start to ignore them as simply a part of the environment.

If you celebrate your little victories each day, you will build the habit like the Olympic motto: *Citius, Altius, Fortius*—faster, higher, stronger. Dr. Fogg admits it may seem silly to give yourself a high five for doing a single push-up or picking up a single piece of clothing from the floor, but that little shot of dopamine you send coursing through your brain with your micro celebration is a lure to future behavior. So, brainstorm with the child ways to celebrate the successful completion of the tiny habit.

If you're looking for ideas for celebration, Fogg has some suggestions. First, you can do a physical action one time. This can be as simple as a finger snap, a single clap, or giving yourself the victory sign or thumbs-up. Or, you can do a more involved physical activity such as a little victory dance, applause, or a hand move more complicated than a single clap or snap. You can use a verbal signal, using common celebration words such as "Good job!" or "I did it!" or "Ta-da!" Celebration sounds are also a good choice. Things like a verbal or tapped out drum roll can signal a little victory.

Singing a line of a song is a great celebration technique. Here are some celebration song suggestions from which you can choose a line or two:

Celebration	by Kool and the Gang
Simply the Best	by Whitney Houston
On Top of the World	by Imagine Dragons
Ain't No Stoppin' Us Now	by McFadden and Whitehead
We Are the Champions	by Queen
Good Feeling	by Flo Rida
All Star	by Smashmouth
How Do You Like Me Now?	by Toby Keith
U Can't Touch This	by MC Hammer
Firework	by Katy Perry

If speaking out loud seems silly, Fogg suggests saying it silently to yourself. This works for songs as well. You can hum a line to yourself. Feel free to combine techniques to create a little celebratory routine.

The Tiny Habits works particularly well with perfectionists for a few reasons. First, many perfectionists tend to set unreasonable and enormous goals for themselves. Breaking things down into very small pieces (Fogg's "Smallest Behavior That Matters") can disrupt that habit. Secondly, one of the negative consequences of perfectionism discussed in Chapter 2 was losing the ability to be satisfied with effort, even if it is at a very high level. Using the Tiny Habit method can return you to the healthier state where you can feel satisfaction with reasonable efforts. Yet another reason Tiny Habits works well with perfectionists is because it ensures the child feels a victory at least one time every day.

Fogg himself is a living metaphor for how to be a high ability, high achiever without the burden of perfectionism. He unapologetically says he's not writing a book about Tiny Habits because he has other projects he wants to do, and he can't do everything. He uses multiple websites to share his information because that works best for him, and he unabashedly admits they're not always up-to-date. At the same time, he's a sought-after speaker, a Stanford professor, has given a TED talk, and produces amazing quantities of work. In addition to his Tiny Habits, perfectionists can use Fogg's own personal habits to model how one can best achieve when perfect not the goal.

The Role of Mental Framework

As an English teacher, I spent a full lesson explaining the idea of "schema" to students. Schema is the unique collection of experiences and knowledge that each person has gathered during their lives through formal and informal means. Schema creates a paradigm through which we understand and interpret new information. Obviously, as we learn and experience more, our schema will change. Understanding our own schema helps us to interpret our experiences accurately. Because "schema" is an unfamiliar word to most people, I often use instead the term "mental framework" when talking with youth. Strategies for helping kids understand how to enjoy the journey, set appropriate goals, and be reasonable about those goals include helping them build the type of mental framework that leads to appropriate perseverance.

A child's mental framework or schema can be influenced dramatically by perfectionism. When Brianna was a high school freshman, her perfectionism became debilitating. In addition to dropping all of her pre-AP classes, she withdrew from orchestra and tennis, both of which she had participated in for years. She stopped attending synagogue with her family, and avoided spending time with one of her oldest friends. Her entire life changed, virtually overnight. Her parents were extremely concerned and eventually found their way to a counselor who began to work through the issues that led Brianna to essentially check out of the life she had been leading.

One mistake her parents had made was in believing that a singular event had sparked Brianna's choices. Although that was a reasonable assumption to make because a drastic move—junior high to high school—had occurred at the same time, it was not an accurate assessment. A few months with the counselor helped to uncover that the timing was correlative, but not causative. Brianna's rejection of nearly all of the components of her life had much deeper roots. She had a schema (a mental framework) she had been building for years, beginning from the time she was very young. One day in a counseling session, Brianna told the counselor that her earliest memory was overhearing her grandmother bragging to someone about how smart Brianna was because she could do a complicated puzzle. She was three years old.

As Brianna grew, she developed a mental framework that all of her activities, relationships, and school experiences existed to make her family proud of her by demonstrating to everyone how smart and successful she was. As you can guess, perfectionism was her constant companion. In eighth grade, her advanced English class read the novel *A Separate Peace* by John Knowles. During the summer, Brianna thought again and again of the character Gene who ruined his life and ended up being responsible for the death of his best friend because he was dishonest with himself. She copied the last lines of the book, "All of them, all except Phineas, constructed at infinite cost to themselves these Maginot Lines against this enemy they thought they saw across the frontier, this enemy who never attacked that way—if he ever attacked at all; if he was indeed the enemy."[25]

Taping the quote to her dresser mirror, she pondered it as the weeks of the summer went by. Her Maginot Line, she realized, was perfectionism, which demonstrated incredible self-awareness for a child her age. Although her insight was mature, her response was not. She decided the only solution was to essentially erase her life and start over. She was going to try to create a new mental framework rather than remodel her existing one. The counselor helped her realize that she could back away from perfectionism yet still maintain the structures of her life, if they were working for her. After discussions with her parents, her rabbi, her high school guidance counselor, and her therapist, Brianna made some decisions. She signed up for two pre-AP classes at the semester break, along with tennis. She began attending synagogue again with her family. She chose not to return to orchestra or attempt to renew the friendship she had discarded. She told the counselor, "I like her a lot, but the relationship is competitive, which just isn't good for me right now."

Brianna is not unique in being strongly affected by mental framework. Adults must help children vocalize their mental frameworks to help them make sure they are accurate. Even very bright children can misinterpret the behaviors, actions, and motives of others. Most of us are susceptible to what is called *confirmation bias*, where we have a tendency to interpret events and words in a way that confirms what we already believe in our mental framework. This is dangerous, as we're often incorrect!

Overcoming perfectionism usually requires a lot of dialogue with the child. In fact, it continues into adulthood, when it often becomes an internal dialogue with oneself. Everyone needs reflection and self-examination to avoid having unhealthy mental frameworks. Effective schema doesn't just appear. It must be nurtured and developed. In addition to effective self-talk and reflection about schema, setting goals and developing grit are parts of developing a healthy mental framework to protect against unhealthy perfectionism

The Role of Mindset

One mental framework that has garnered a lot of attention is the work of Carol Dweck in what she terms "mindset." In essence, the mindset theory says that there are two basic mindsets—fixed and growth. People with fixed mindsets believe their ability is fixed and that challenge is an opportunity for failure and humiliation. People with a growth mindset, on the other hand, believe that their ability is fluid and malleable. They see challenge as an opportunity for growth. Clearly, growth mindset is the more desirable one to have. When we can face problems with an attitude of learning and growing, we develop a healthier mental framework, and we are likely to be able to develop our abilities and skills to a higher degree.

Although the term "mindset" is quickly becoming overused and the ideas behind it oversimplified, I recommend Dweck's book *Mindset: The New Psychology of Success*, but not the books about mindset that are written for youth because they discourage parents and teachers from telling kids they're gifted. I believe in honesty with youth, and it doesn't help to withhold information from people about themselves. The kids already know they're different, whether we give a name to it or not. In the same way I'd tell my child if she had diabetes, I'll tell her she has high cognitive abilities. She didn't earn it or ask for it—it's just part of who she is, and she'll live a healthier life if she knows what's involved in being different in that way. I also believe that it stigmatizes giftedness to withhold it. Avoiding use of the term gifted implies an underlying discomfort and an assumption that suggests that using the term will turn kids into arrogant, socially backward individuals who commit *faux pas* at birthday parties, or encourage the belief that they are somehow a better species of human simply because they were born wired differently than many other children.

I understand that the rationale in the mindset camp is to avoid the dynamic where the child feels that things should come easily because of the giftedness, but not telling a child is too drastic a move to accomplish that, in my opinion. It also assumes that the only rationale response to finding out that one has high cognitive ability is a fixed mindset in which we believe that it is only intelligence that is responsible for our success. That is a false assumption. Parents can easily send the message that this is not true; high ability is a starting point, not a destiny.

The Role of Grit

A few years ago, I contacted a professor at the University of Pennsylvania, to request an interview for an article I was writing. She turned me down (nicely), saying she was too busy with her research to talk with journalists. I was so flattered to be called a journalist that I risked a second reach-out. I had watched her TED talk, and I knew she had a daughter. Assuming the child was bright, I offered a trade—my gifted expertise vis-à-vis her daughter for insight into her work. She agreed, and I still remember with a smile the half hour I spent on the phone with Angela Duckworth, famous for her work with what she calls "grit." Grit is perseverance and passion in pursuit of a long-term goal. It's the antithesis of a fixed mindset. Grit encompasses determination, stick-with-it-ness, and a host of other traits that mean that we don't give up prematurely.

When I first read Duckworth's work, it reminded me of a talk I'd heard by Olympic gymnast Peter Vidmar. Peter was a member of the men's Olympic gymnastics team that won gold in 1984 at the games held in Los Angeles. In his inspirational talk, Vidmar shared a lesson he learned from his coach when he was a young gymnast leaving for his first national team training camp. His coach didn't tell him to be better than everyone, to outperform the other gymnasts, or to show off. His send-off request was that Peter return from the camp able to tell the coach honestly that he had worked harder than anyone else.

Peter went to the camp, following his coach's request. He determined to be the last one out of the gym each day. He would do more exercises in his room when others were relaxing with pizza and beer. He didn't, though, work ridiculously harder. You can only train so much every day. Vidmar says the difference was working five minutes more or going the extra hundred yards. That's grit. It's the mental framework that says, "I'm going to stick with this five more minutes. I'm going to practice a smidge harder. I'm going to work a little harder today than I did yesterday."[26]

In exploring grit and the scale created to measure it, Duckworth and her colleagues[27] visited some pretty gritty places, like West Point and the Scripps Spelling Bee. What they found was that even in these very competitive, high-performance environments, grit played a key role in success. The mental framework that presupposes things will be hard and long is not a mental framework in which perfectionism easily grows. It recognizes the role of effort, not just ability.

What mindset and grit have in common is the idea that it's not just about doing this thing that's fun right now, but rather being in it for the long term. It's about finding things that take a long time to master, like piano or other musical instruments. It's about learning another language.

Sure, you can learn a few words very quickly (make it a Tiny Habit!), but it takes years to develop true fluency. Adults can encourage kids to choose to engage in hobbies and pursuits that can't be accomplished in just a month or two, but instead take years to master. We can help them choose appropriate goals and activities, and guide them as they develop habits associated with grit.

Goal Disengagement

One key to avoiding perfectionism during childhood is understanding and implementing healthy goal disengagement, the term used for recognizing an inappropriate goal, leaving it, and choosing a different goal instead. A common dynamic in perfectionistic individuals is to latch onto a goal, even one that doesn't work for them, and never let go. When this happens, frustration grows, and perfectionists often think that if they just did the thing better, the goal itself would become the right goal, rather than accepting that the best choice may be to disengage from the current goal and commit to a different one.

When Isaac was in fourth grade, many of his friends began playing baseball in an organized league. Isaac wanted to play as well, so his mom signed him up. At first, he loved it, especially the after-practice snacks his mom gave him. After a month or so, however, the twice-weekly practices, along with games on Saturdays, began to be less appealing. Getting out the door increasingly became a struggle, and after a couple of months, Isaac told his mom he wanted to quit baseball. His mom, who had spent over $100 on cleats and other equipment as well as the registration fee, was annoyed. She told him he couldn't just quit. "I don't want you to turn into a quitter," she told him, and insisted that he continue. Every practice and game was a battle. His friends on the team stopped liking Isaac, as his frustration grew, and he made it abundantly clear that he didn't want to play. His comments like, "Baseball is stupid," didn't endear him to his teammates. The next year, when he wanted to play soccer, his mom said no. She had no interest in repeating the debacle of the year before.

While not an uncommon scenario, this situation is almost always avoidable. An important but often overlooked aspect of setting goals is goal disengagement. When you become aware that a goal has lost its usefulness or practicality, you disengage from that goal and then reengage in a new goal. Now, this may seem like it conflicts with the idea of grit, but it is compatible. Grit doesn't mean sticking with a goal that doesn't work for you or beyond the time it is helpful to you. How do you balance these ideas, both of which are best practices? One solution is to share with a child that joining an activity, whether it's a sport, arts, or social activity, is like driving your car onto the freeway. When you get on a freeway, occasionally you will realize you're actually going the wrong direction— going east instead of west. You can't simply stop in the middle of the freeway and start going the other way. You have to wait until the nearest safe exit. Freeways often have turn-arounds for emergencies, but in general, you stay on until it is safe to get off. The same is true of sports, specialized classes, or other extra-curricular activities. Once involved, the child needs to remain until the next logical exit (end of the season, semester break, can play piano with both hands simultaneously, etc.). Together with the child, decide what the logical exit is. If the child can commit to give the activity a chance until then, then feel free to move forward with a new direction.

The length of time that constitutes a reasonable commitment is going to vary depending upon the activity and the age of the child. Parents have to back away from their own emotions and agendas, and certainly don't want to get in such a power struggle that it wrecks the relationship with the child. If a child has been playing cello for eight or nine years and comes to you saying, "I don't want to play cello anymore," it can be difficult to dial back our desire to think about all the money invested, the time spent in practice, how you are the treasurer of the booster club, and how you have paid for years of orchestra trips. All of that is what economists would call a sunk cost. Sunk costs are costs that have already been incurred and cannot be recovered. You've already spent the money; the benefit has already been obtained.

Forcing children to continue in something that is not right for them at that time because of sunk costs in money or time fosters perfectionism, and I speak from personal experience. When my son quit violin, it was painful. I was sorely tempted to argue that we had spent lots of money of lessons, that he would regret it, that the violin was expensive, and on and on. That was not the right thing to do, however. His interests had changed. He had taken his study of violin as far as made sense for him. Recently, I saw him list hobbies and he didn't even include violin, even though in the past, he had played solos during concerts. It clearly wasn't right for him anymore, and I had to be okay with that. As parents and teachers, we have to back off of the idea that simply because a child is capable of doing something (and doing it well) the child should be expected to do it. Gifted children by definition have many abilities, and if the adults around them send the message explicitly or obliquely that they should do everything they are capable of doing, the result may be perfectionism.

If the child is too young to commit, then you may need to carefully consider if the child is old enough for an organized activity. One reason we end up with children quitting activities is that we sometimes put them in organized, adult-supervised activities too early, making it impossible for children to know if they want to do the activity in a formal setting or not. Do not feel pressured to enroll children in formal programs when they are young. Casual participation is fine, and often preferable. In Isaac's case, when he expressed interest in playing baseball, a useful conversation would be a series of questions to find out why he wanted to play. Does he really like baseball, or does he want more time with his friends? If what he really wants is time with friends, then the pressured drill of team practices could do more harm than good. If he did want to play, explaining that a sport is a commitment for an entire season and coming to agreement on that before play begins would be helpful in avoiding the dynamic that unfolded.

Research shows that the happiest people are able to abandon unattainable goals and reengage in valued alternative goals.[28] Goal disengagement can only work if the person is aware of available alternative goals, so part of our role as adults is to help youth decide if goals are working for them and to identify more appropriate goals in which to reengage. Goal disengagement is a skill that helps with perfectionism. In one study, the researchers suggested that having new goals ready at the wings and reengaging quickly in those new goals reduces the negative consequences of abandoning the first goal because the person is still engaged in activities of value. This has particular application for parents, because if we channel kids too early into an identity as one particular thing (football player, gymnast, pianist, etc.) and then the child becomes disinterested or the thing becomes unattainable or inappropriate for whatever reason, it can be demoralizing to the child.

Goals, grit, and mindset are all part of a journey-oriented, anti-perfectionism strategy. When adults share the ideas of using goals as a way to create a journey of wonder and growth, rather than as a way to prove one's worth, youth are better able to grow into the idea that we engage in challenging activities to enrich our lives, not to prove that we are perfect. Youth and adults who can set appropriate goals, pursue them appropriately, and yet disengage if the goal is not useful, lead happier lives that are less susceptible to the pressures of perfectionism. Like Odysseus, they can make it through even difficult trials, knowing the goal will serve them well because it is the goals that provide the journey.

Key Ideas:

- The purpose of goals is to provide a journey experience.
- Adults should help youth set appropriate goals.
- Doing a cost-benefit analysis of goals can be more helpful than a pro/con list.
- The Tiny Habit strategy can be an effective way to move toward a goal in a healthy, non-perfectionistic way.
- A child's mental framework has a strong impact on decisions and goals.
- An understanding of Mindset and Grit can help parents and teachers assist youth in achieving their goals.
- Goal disengagement is a key to having healthy relationship with goals.

Action Steps:

- With the child, identify current goals and the journey those goals are providing.
- In setting future goals, use a cost-benefit analysis to determine if the goal is a good choice at that time.
- Using Fogg's Tiny Habit strategy, help the child identify and implement a Tiny Habit.
- Read either Dweck's Mindset or Duckworth's Grit, and discuss the ideas with your child or students.
- Consider if any current goals are not working for the child. Discuss the ideas of goal disengagement and help identify alternate goals, if appropriate.
- For future goals, in addition to the cost-benefit analysis, decide on an appropriate time to disengage and commit to at least that point.

The Importance of Developing an Effective Self-Concept

We adore perfection because we can't have it; it would disgust us if we had it. Perfect is inhuman, because human is imperfect.

- FERNANDO PESSOA

One of the great ironies of perfectionism is that perfectionists can come across to others as arrogant, stuck-up, and hyper-driven. From the outside, they look like self-absorbed narcissists who are convinced they hung the moon. The reality is that perfectionists are often self-loathing and insecure. The stress that accompanies perfectionism alters personalities. No one is her best self under constant stress, and that is true even if you are five years old. The greatest defense against this dynamic is the development of an effective self-concept, often called self-esteem, in the way we view ourselves. With an effective self-concept, a person has a realistic view of strengths and weakness and accepts them.

A perfectionists' self-concept is often warped, skewed, or tied up completely in their ability to perform tasks perfectly or at least better than everyone else. Because no one is perfect, self-concept is often lower than is emotionally healthy in a perfectionist. While people who don't struggle with perfectionism develop their self-concept in several ways, for perfectionists, it's often a one-note symphony. Ironically, that increases perfectionistic tendencies, as the person struggles to be ever more perfect to try to build his sense of self. Failing to achieve perfection, the self-concept goes even lower, leading to an increase in perfectionistic behavior, and so on. Therefore, the development of a healthy, effective self-concept is key to avoiding, or at least minimizing, perfectionism.

The Poker Chip Metaphor

In *100 Ways to Enhance Self-Concept*,[29] the authors use the following analogy: A person's' self-esteem is like a stack of poker chips, and each person has a different amount. As we face challenges in our lives, we lose chips. As we experience successes, we gain them. The more chips we have, the more loss we are able to sustain. Therefore, people with fewer chips are less willing to take risks because they can't afford the loss. This makes sense, doesn't it? Imagine that we went to Las Vegas to gamble. We sit down at a poker table with a large stack of chips piled before us. We are dealt a mediocre hand, but we are undaunted because we have so many chips in front of us. Despite this less-than-stellar hand, we shove a pile of chips toward the center of the table. We take risks because we can afford it.

When people suffer from perfectionistic tendencies, it is as if there is a gaping hole on the table before them, and no matter how many chips pile up, they quickly disappear down the hole. For this reason, developing a strong self-concept is the first line of defense to protect against perfectionism. It covers up the hole, allowing the person to retain chips and continue to take risks—risks that are needed if a person is to grow. If we build our children's stack of self-esteem poker chips, we enable them to take healthy and appropriate risks in our classrooms and in their lives in general.

Measuring Self-Esteem

You need not worry that you are going to create an arrogant monster. In an American Association of University Women (AAUW) study called *Shortchanging Girls, Shortchanging America*, 3,000 girls and boys were asked to agree or disagree with this statement: "I'm happy the way I am."[30] The results were startling. In elementary school, 67% of boys and 60% of girls agreed with the statement. By high school, those numbers declined. Only 46% of boys and 29% percent of girls said that they are satisfied with themselves. The low high school numbers may distract from the elementary statistics. Viewed another way, if 67% of elementary school boys say they are happy the way they are, that means that more than three in ten are not happy with themselves, and the numbers are worse for the girls. This kind of dissatisfaction fuels perfectionism, as young people try to be more and more perfect in an attempt to feel better about themselves.

The AAUW study used the *Self-Esteem Index*, an instrument used by mental health professionals to measure five areas of basic, individual self-esteem. The five-point Likert scale (strongly agree, agree, neutral, disagree, strongly disagree), asks people to agree or disagree with 80 statements such as:

- I like the way I look.
- I like most things about myself.
- I'm happy the way I am.
- Sometimes I don't like myself that much.
- I wish I were someone else.

The biggest difference in self-esteem between girls and boys centered on the subject of "doing things." Boys were much more likely than girls to feel "pretty good at doing a lot of things." Almost half the boys rated this statement as always true, compared to less than a third of the girls, and the boys' sense of confidence in their ability to "do things" correlated strongly with general self-confidence.

We may think that youth who are struggling with perfectionism would agree strongly that they are pretty good at doing things. After all, they usually do things very, very well. However, in their self-evaluation, the opposite is true. Most perfectionists feel a deep sense of inadequacy.

Girls, even though they have a wide range of skills and are confident in being able to do things, nonetheless have lower overall self-concept. Because girls are more likely to be praised for appearance than skill acquisition, they can lose out on the self-concept boost that feeling confidence in having a wide range of skills gives.

As we look at the role of self-concept vis-à-vis perfectionism, it seems clear that self-concept is rooted in feelings of competence—feeling like you are pretty good (not perfect) at actually *doing* things. This is different from feeling like you are pretty good at *being* things or maintaining an image. It turns out that no amount of "you look pretty" can equal "I know how to do that" for building self-concept.

Societal Pressure

In Shakespeare's play, *Henry V*, the son of the king of France tells Henry, "Self-love, my liege, is not so vile a sin as self-neglecting." Unfortunately, in our culture, this is not a commonly held belief. We overvalue false modesty and self-deprecation, and we undervalue self-confidence. If someone says, "I'm good at *xyz*," the person is often labeled as arrogant or stuck-up. Even if someone else gives the compliment, the receiver is often expected to respond in a way to deflect the compliment by saying something like, "Oh, it was easy" or "You didn't see the picture of how it was supposed to be." This dynamic works against gifted children. Since society doesn't approve of people's talking about their strengths, people feel that a child's saying, "I'm smart" or "I'm a good thinker" is bragging or being arrogant. Parents of gifted children often feel that they cannot celebrate their child's achievements without risking the rolled eyes and judgment of others. Interestingly, this is not true of athletics, where we praise and worship the highest achievers.

Part of the reason girls are less likely than boys to gain self-esteem from accomplishment in doing things is because our culture focuses on a woman's appearance as her primary trait of value and worth. One large survey, called *Beauty Redefined*,[31] found that nine in ten teenage girls said that the fashion industry and/or the media place a lot of pressure on girls to be thin. While they recognize these industries are putting undue (and often unhealthy) pressure on them, three-quarters feel that fashion is very important if they are to be "perfect." The relentless societal pressure prompts only 10% of Caucasian teenage girls to feel totally satisfied with their bodies. The numbers are slightly better for Hispanic girls (14%) and African American girls (17%). When body dissatisfaction brushes up against perfectionism, eating disorders, unhealthy relationships, and other negative behaviors can come into play.

The pressures are not solely on girls. Recently, when I asked a group of gifted teenage boys if they felt pressured to look a certain way, nearly three-quarters of them said yes. As one seventeen-year-old boy said, "Now I feel like I can't just get good grades. I also have to be super strong and I'm supposed to shave off the hair on my chest. It's like I'll never be enough."

Parents and educators can counteract this pressure in ways that diminish perfectionism through clear dialogue, discussing the ways people try to match the expectations from others around them. The appearance pressure is so strong that people often engage in unhealthy practices, and if they feel powerless to counteract that pressure, it's a place where perfectionism can be particularly damaging.

Building effective self-concept to counteract societal pressures is not as tricky as it may seem, so don't feel discouraged. Here are five keys to effectively develop self-concept to help youth (and adults) build the kind of self-esteem that is protective against perfectionism and other negative consequences of low self-esteem as well.

Five Keys to Building Self-Concept

A Sense of Inherent Self-Worth. Youth must have an unshakeable belief in their inherent self-worth. This is perhaps the most difficult of all of the keys because it must come from inside them with little guidance. It comes only when we ask youth to do things that are vastly different from the typical self-absorbed activities we expect of most youth. Playing endless hours of video games and flicking through Instagram may be fun ways to pass time, but to build a strong sense of self-worth, passing time is not the goal—seizing time meaningfully is.

In 1943, an intelligent and vibrant Hungarian young woman named Hannah Szenes (usually anglicized "Senesh"), living in then-British controlled Palestine, enlisted in the British Army in the Women's Auxiliary Air Force and was trained as a paratrooper. In early 1944, after her training was completed, Hannah and two colleagues parachuted into what was then Yugoslavia, discovering too late that the Germans had beaten them there. Hannah was captured at the Hungarian border, taken to prison, and tortured in an attempt to gain the code to her British radio transmitter. Despite brutal treatment, Hannah refused to break, likely saving the life of her mother, who was arrested as leverage against Hannah.

While in prison, she signaled to other prisoners using a mirror to flash signals and large cut out letters she held up one at a time to her cell window. Hannah wrote poetry throughout her captivity, until she was tried for treason and executed by firing squad in November of 1944, just months before the end of the war. In the diary she kept from age thirteen until her death, Hannah wrote, "One needs something to believe in, something for which one can have wholehearted enthusiasm. One needs to feel that one's life has meaning, that one is needed in this world."[32]

People, even in childhood, do not develop this strength of character by living a life completely devoted to enjoyment and entertainment. On the afternoon of December 3, 1935, Dr. Albert Schweitzer arrived at Silcoates School in Wakefield, West Yorkshire, England, to give a speech he called "The Meaning of Ideals in Life."[33] As Dr. Schweitzer began to talk to the gathered students, he didn't give a rousing, team-building speech on how wonderful they were. Instead, he made a prediction. "I don't know what your destiny will be, but one thing I know. The only ones among you who will be truly happy are those who will have sought and found how to serve others."

He warned them against looking for big, fancy ways to serve. Rather, he encouraged them to more humble, personal service. He advised them, "You see somebody alone—try and be with him, try to give him some of the hours which you might take for yourself and in that way learn to serve; and then only will you begin to find true happiness." The happiness Schweitzer promised those youths on that cold, grey day in England was the happiness that comes when you feel the way Hannah Szenes described—when you have the sense of purpose that comes only through devotion to something outside of yourself.

It's ironic, isn't it, that the thing virtually guaranteed to make us feel better about ourselves is to step outside of ourselves? And yet, it's true. When we feel better about ourselves from authentic sources such as commitment to a cause larger than ourselves, we are far less likely to become obsessed with getting everything just right. Seeing the broader world directs focus through a window, rather than into a mirror. When we're focused on others, we have less energy, time, and inclination to fixate on ourselves, which protects against perfectionism.

During the times I have felt the lowest in my life, service to others has been a lifeline that has saved me from despair. When we help our children learn this very early on, when we encourage their service to others even in small and private ways, as well as in partnership with others, we solidify their own self-worth. With young children, we start small, with little acts of kindness towards others. We can share with them the things we are doing to help others so that they know that this is just a part of who we are. Later, their own interests may lead them to service on a larger scale.

When Will Lourcey, a member of my local MENSA˚ chapter, was seven years old, he felt bothered after seeing a man beg for food on the side of the road, and decided to do something about it. He rallied his baseball teammates to form "FROGS"—Friends Reaching Our Goals[34] to begin raising money for the county food bank, with donations coming through pledges for hits and runs. As the program grew, donations provided over 200,000 meals to the food bank (not a typo!). Will, who was named a CNN Young Wonder Hero, was later featured on Nickelodeon's *The Halo Effect*, and has won many other grants and awards. As Will said at the Jefferson Foundation Awards dinner, "I saw a need, made a plan, gathered friends, and set out to change the world."

Through his efforts on behalf of others. Will learned that he is needed, and the support of his parents helped Will in his determination. His mother Julie has spent many hours filling the family SUV with food, traveling the country with Will as he makes speeches, and supports him through her willingness to prioritize his passion for service. Youth often need help in serving, and not just for transportation. They may need ideas, as well. As a teacher, I have partnered my class with a Peace Corps volunteer through the World Wise Schools program,[35] and we have made micro loans around the world through Kiva,[36] an online micro lending community. We've made alphabet books for children in the lower grades, and we've visited the cafeteria to thank the workers for their efforts on our behalf. When we make service a part of the way we do things, self-concept follows as a natural consequence. Life looks different when you know people are relying on you in the best of ways.

Jane Bluestein discusses the role of service in combatting perfectionism. "Sometimes the best way to get out of our own head and disconnect from our problems and stress is by doing service for others," she suggests. "Giving of our imperfect selves—a kind word, courteous gesture, or a genuine smile can change the world."[37] Note the emphasis on making sure we're not trying to be perfect in our service, as that can make perfectionism worse.

When youth fully engage in authentic opportunities to serve others, the perfectionism dynamic begins to shift, and realizing that no one in the world has a perfect life is a part of this shift. Youth who reach outside of themselves expend intense emotional energy that they otherwise often focus on themselves. Instead of worrying about what people are thinking about them or worrying about their inability to be exactly how they wish they were, they become mentally busier thinking about what they have done to affect positive change in the world and what they have the opportunity to do. Making a loan of $25 to a poor shopkeeper in Ghana turns out to be more important in protecting against perfectionism than logic would indicate. Being needed in the world, with all of your imperfections, is powerful medicine.

Self-Awareness. When Layla was in fifth grade, her teacher overheard her saying to another student, "You're so good at that. I'm not good at anything!" The teacher spoke privately with Layla soon after to ask her about what that remark. During the conversation, it was clear that Layla easily recognized the accomplishments of others, but not herself. When reminded that she had won an award the year before for an essay she had written, she said, "Yeah, but that was easy because I like to write." She attributed others' accomplishments to skill, and her own to luck. Like so many of us, Layla discounted and minimized things that came easy to her; she focused instead on the things she could not do as easily, and used those as a yardstick for measuring her abilities.

Using a technique he had learned from a professional development session, her teacher had her make a Pride Line—a list of things we've accomplished that we're proud of. It isn't just a brag list, and it has some guidelines. The Pride Line is a list of statements that begin, "I was proud of myself when…" It consists of things that are specific, rather than a generic list of talents and achievements. For example, "I was proud of myself when I shared the last cookie with DeOndre," or "I was proud of myself when I spent ten extra minutes cleaning up my room to make sure it was neat for my grandmother's visit." The things need not be big; in fact, it's better if they're not. Self-concept builds best in small increments over time. That way, if one accomplishment is diminished in some way, it doesn't make as big of an impact. The Pride Line also focuses on an action, not a quality. Rather than writing, "I'm a nice person" or "I was kind," write, "I sat by Juanita in the cafeteria so she wouldn't sit alone" or "I invited the new kid to my birthday party." A simple, inexpensive spiral notebook makes a great place to keep a Pride Line. It becomes a journal of sorts, and reviewing it can help youth become more self-aware of their skills and value, particularly when they are feeling dejected because the negative self-talk of perfectionism has reared its ugly head. Youth who are more digitally minded can use a memo feature on a phone or tablet.

Symbols of success help build self-awareness as well, and are even more powerful when they are displayed. When my children were small, I had surgery that went horribly wrong. I was in the hospital for a month in very bad shape, with fourteen inches of incision slashing across my abdomen. While there, my middle son had his 10th birthday. Oh, how I love to throw birthday parties for my kids, but that year, it was modestly done by my husband—miniature golf and arcade games at a local establishment with a cake from Costco. My husband brought the kids to see me at the hospital after the party, and my youngest son, Joseph, said, "Mama, I have someping for you" (he had a little speech impediment). He pulled out a gold-painted, plastic, articulated robot. It was quite possibly the ugliest thing I have seen before or since. He beamed with pride. "I got it wif my tickets! It's for your IV pole!" he said excitedly. I could only imagine what people would think seeing that thing hanging from my IV pole, but I had my husband hook it up for me before they left.

A weird thing about hospitals is that even though it costs so much to stay there, they don't like you to stay in your bed very long. The nurses constantly urged me to walk, but I didn't like to. My hair was lank and stringy. My hospital gown was hard to keep closed. My stomach hurt so badly that I couldn't stand straight up, so I walked hunched over. Every step was torture. However, I knew I had to walk in order to regain my health. After my family left, I ventured out of my room, gold robot swinging conspicuously with every step. As I passed a man coming out of another room, he pointed at the robot and said, "I'll bet they charge a lot extra for that." A few feet farther, another patient asked, "Did you get that beauty in the gift shop?"

Before my robot, I found being in the hospital isolating and lonely. Once I had my swinging robot, I began to look forward to my walks, no matter how painful they were physically, because people talked to me when I had it. I began walking more and more, and I recovered my strength and was able to return home to my family, scarred but alive. That gold plastic robot I was so unimpressed with when Joseph pulled it out of his pocket hangs in a place of pride in my closet where I see it every day. It isn't a trophy. It isn't a certificate or award. But it is my dearest success symbol. It reminds me every single day that I have faced harder things than I will face that day, and that I can face whatever comes my way.

The things your child needs around as reminders of successes don't have to be beautiful or expensive. They only need to be authentic reminders of battles hard fought and hard won. These symbols may not mean anything to someone who doesn't know the story, but that is unimportant. What is important is that they mean something to the person. When we have reminders around us of times when we conquered difficult challenges or succeeded when we thought we would fail (or at first *did* fail), we gather courage to not be perfect in our futures. Tangible reminders of our skills and achievements are far more effective than the praise of others in preventing the risk avoidance so common in perfectionism.

Connection. Connecting with others decreases perfectionism because as we get to know others, we can see that everyone has flaws, everyone has strengths and weaknesses, and no one achieves their goals all of the time. We gain a more realistic expectation of ourselves by deeper relationships with others.

On the other hand, gifted children's connections and interactions with others, fueled by their intensity, may make them more likely to have higher self-expectations. Gifted children frequently are drawn to older children or adults who may be more likely to share interests that are different from children their own age, and this can inspire them to think more broadly and deeply. The true peers of gifted children may not be their same age, but rather older children or adults who share similar interests, abilities, or motivation. However, as psychologist Maureen Neihart notes, also "their advanced maturity means that they often have different expectations for friendships, looking for intimacy and moral integrity at much earlier ages than other children."[38]

Because connection is critical to minimizing perfectionism, it's important that adults in the child's life understand this dynamic of friendship so that they can help facilitate building those connections, yet simultaneously help youngsters avoid believing that they should be as competent in tasks as the older children or adults.

Parents need to consider their expectations for the child's peer interaction, and, as the child matures, discuss these with the child. For children who struggle with face-to-face contact, pen pals are a good way to connect, along with digital platforms. Another possibility is the care of a pet. Relationships with animals are powerful in the lives of children and adults, and caring for a pet can develop core values of compassion and concern for others. While it is a rare child who gets along with *all* children (I mean, do you?), everyone can gain insight into the behavior and feelings of others. As we do, we improve our own self-concept.

It is also important that parents and educators not undermine gifted children's social comfort by consciously or unwittingly expecting that simply because a child is gifted, he or she will be socially awkward. The research simply does not bear this out. Children of all intellectual levels struggle with peer acceptance, and adults often exacerbate the situation in several ways. When parents or educators assume that a gifted child is likely to have social difficulties, they often use coincidental experiences to confirm the hypothesis, even when similar incidents among typical learners would not generate the same conclusion.

Occasionally, adults will use social difficulty, age-group peer awkwardness, or maladaptive behaviors simply as signs of profound giftedness. Because of this misguided thinking, they may not intervene to help the child acquire appropriate social skills as they would in a typical learner. In extreme cases, they unintentionally may subtly encourage it, implying to others that a lack of social appropriateness on their child's part is simply part of his or her giftedness. This dynamic prevents connection with peers, particularly if the child internalizes the message that it is the giftedness that distances him or her from peers, rather than needing to develop a skill that is lacking. I have had to say many times, "Appropriate behavior does not stifle IQ, nor is inappropriate behavior proof of giftedness."

When Christina, who was quite advanced intellectually, started Kindergarten, trouble arose almost immediately. She was impatient with peers, refused to take turns, and was disrespectful to her teacher in ways that bordered on cruelty. One day, as a classmate practiced a list of sight words, Christina sighed heavily and loudly proclaimed, "I can't believe I have to be in class with people who are so stupid." Christina's teacher, who was trained about giftedness, requested a conference, but was quickly dismayed by Christina's parents' lack of understanding or insight about the social behavior of gifted children.

The teacher began by sharing Christina's strengths, including her care and compassion for the classroom pets. She asked the parents about any concerns they had, and then she shared her concerns about Christina's behavior towards her and other students. "That's just because she's gifted," Christina's dad told the teacher. "Gifted children are impatient with others who aren't as smart as they are."

Christina's teacher tried to explain that Christina was welcome to feel impatience, but that there were acceptable and unacceptable ways of showing that impatience. Neither of Christina's parents were swayed.

"We're not going to force her to behave in a way that works for you. That would deny her giftedness. It's part of who she is," Christina's mother told the teacher. "The more gifted you are, the more different your behavior is from others'."

The teacher who told me this story at a conference expected that I would be surprised. I was not. I have seen this dynamic many times, in which parents feel as though inappropriate behavior is a sign of high intelligence. I asked the teacher what she had done, and she said that the parents had decided to withdraw their daughter from the school.

I have had to say many times, "Appropriate behavior does not have a depressive effect upon IQ, nor is inappropriate behavior proof of giftedness."

Occasionally adults will use social difficulty as a misguided diagnostic tool, seeing age-group peer awkwardness or maladaptive behavior as a sign of profound giftedness. Because of this, they may not intervene to help the child acquire appropriate social skills as they would in a typical learner. In extreme cases, they may actually subtly encourage it, intimating to others that a lack of social appropriateness on their child's part is simply part of his or her giftedness. This dynamic prevents connection with peers because the child may internalize the message that it is the giftedness that distances him or her from peers, rather than normal social development strain or a skill that is lacking but could be developed.

Parents may reflect upon what their expectations are for peer interaction, and, as the child matures, discuss these with the child. For children who struggle with face-to-face contact, pen pals are a good way to connect, along with digital platforms. Another possibility is the care of a pet. Relationships with animals are powerful in the lives of children and adults. While it is a rare child who gets along with all children (I mean, do you?), everyone can gain insight into the behavior and feelings of others. As we do, we improve our own self-concept.

Understanding Practice and Effort. It isn't easy to become truly great at any challenging task, and we do a disservice to children if we allow them to think that it is. If you think that because you're smart, you should find being excellent at something easy, perfectionism grows. You may not know Anders Ericsson by name, but you have likely heard of his work. Ericsson, a professor at Florida State University, studies expert performance, and it is his research that has led to the idea of the "10,000 Hour Rule." Essentially, the 10,000 Hour Rule says that it takes 10,000 hours of deliberate practice to develop expertise in most fields.

In his study, "The Role of Deliberate Practice in the Acquisition of Expert Performance,"[39] Ericsson studied violinists at the Berlin Academy of Music. He divided them into three groups, depending upon level of skill, with those destined to became virtuoso performers at the top. Ericsson set out to discover what separated those top-level performers from less skilled players. He asked all of the music students, "Over the course of your entire career, ever since you first picked up the violin, how many hours have you practiced?" Although they had all begun playing around the age of five, something happened around the age of eight that separated them from the other levels of violinists. A great divergence appeared in the amount that they practiced. Ericsson found the same pattern when he looked at pianists and chess masters and athletes. For those who became truly expert, what distinguished themselves from their peers was not natural ability, but rather practice. The amazing ones had practiced much harder than the others.

In his book, *Outliers*, Malcolm Gladwell writes, "The striking thing about Ericsson's study is that he and his colleagues couldn't find any 'naturals,' or musicians who floated effortlessly to the top while practicing a fraction of the time their peers did. Nor could they find any 'grinds'— people who worked harder than everyone else, yet just didn't have what it takes to break the top ranks."[40] This flies in the face of the idea that innate talent is the essence of high performance, and that realization is very good news for people trying to overcome perfectionism. Often, people think that because they are smart or have some innate ability, things should come easily to them. When things become difficult and they cannot be "perfect," they quit because they feel discouraged and begin to doubt themselves.

Unfortunately, many people misinterpreted Ericsson's study. The idea was bandied about that after 10,000 hours of practice, anyone could become a master of anything. Not so fast, says Ericsson. We all know that you can golf every weekend and never meaningfully improve your game. I walk my dog every single day, easily for 10,000 hours, yet I'm not an Olympic race walker. Why? Ericsson says that it's not just *any* practice. It's what he calls "deliberate practice." For practice to be deliberate, we must be motivated to improve. My husband golfs to hang out with friends and spend time outside. I walk my dog to keep both of us fit. We're not trying to improve. We're in it for different purposes. If you want to get better, you have to want to get better. You also have to get feedback, and the sooner the better. We work harder for coaches than we do when we're practicing alone, in no small part because they are there giving us feedback in real time.

Additionally, you have to perform the same task again and again. You have to be willing to do the necessary but less-than-exciting work of practicing the small pieces of performance that separate the true artisan from the dabbler. I had a friend whose father was a surgeon. At night, he worked on the strength of his hand by squeezing a tennis ball inside a shoe box over and over. He was one of the foremost surgeons in the country, yet he never stopped practicing the fundamentals. Gifted students often rebel against this, wanting to move on once they feel they can do something well enough. They are less willing than the general population to work at things they feel they know, and that is often true, even of perfectionists.

It's not just Ericsson who argues this point. Daniel Chambliss, in his research study titled the "Mundanity of Excellence"[41] found that swimmers who did the best spent the most time and effort on mundane activities that readied them for races, with slight adjustments here and there, as opposed to massive amounts of more practice time. He learned that what others see as boring—such as swimming back and forth over a black line for two hours—they find peaceful, even meditative, challenging, or therapeutic. They enjoy hard practices, look forward to difficult competitions, and try to set difficult goals. In this way, they turn practice into its own game day. The work of Ericsson and Chambliss shows that we don't practice until we get it right; we practice until we can't get it wrong. Notice the difference here between their expectations and the expectations of most perfectionists; the goals they set were high, but they knew they had to persist, and they were not handicapped or paralyzed if they did not quickly reach their goals.

Another key factor was that expert performers didn't expect to enjoy the practice. They knew the practice was leading them to a goal. For many activities, game days are already built in. Piano recitals, soccer games, martial arts tournaments, parades, and concerts all provide an opportunity to display talent developed in deliberate practice. For parents and teachers, that means we must provide a game day for students. Report cards are not a game day. They are communication between school and home. We need to make sure that we are providing a way to showcase the results of practice. Practice alone is not motivating enough to encourage someone to continue to practice effectively. In addition to work stuck to the fridge with magnets, we can use technology to share work with relatives far away. Even a simple discussion about assignments brought home can provide a mini game day.

High standards and strivings to become an expert does not necessarily mean that a person will suffer the anxieties of perfectionism. Perfectionism is less likely to be an issue for us if we truly and deeply understand and internalize that even people who are very, very good at something may have doubts, but nonetheless work hard for it. Self-doubt is something to be conquered. In Shakespeare's play *Measure for Measure*, he writes, "Our doubts are traitors, and make us lose the good we oft might win by fearing to attempt." Our doubts are traitors to our self-concept, encouraging us to avoid the attempt. Ralph Waldo Emerson said, "That which we persist in doing becomes easier, not that the task itself has become easier, but that our ability to perform it has improved."

When we understand that effective, deliberate practice is the key to success, we are less likely to feel like we are personal failures when things pose a challenge or do not yield to our efforts on the first try. Perfectionism is less likely to be an issue if we understand and internalize that even people who are very, very good at something work hard for it. There is a strong connection between what we know about achievement and the prevention of perfectionism; perfectionism is in large part a disconnect between what we think it takes to do something well and what it really takes.

Valuing Intuition. Seventeen students are in a room taking an AP Comparative Government exam, and the exam is grueling. A tremendous amount of content is covered in a one-semester course, and the exam is typically given on the first day of AP testing. When the exam was over, one of the students came to my room to decompress. "How do you feel like it went?" I asked. "My gut is raw," Kyle said. That was just what I wanted to hear. I didn't want his brain fried, as you might expect: I wanted his gut burned out.

Comparative Government, one of my favorite courses to teach, is tricky because in Advanced Placement courses, you don't prepare students to choose the correct answer from a selection of five answer choices on the multiple-choice section. You prepare them to choose the *best* answer from four correct answers, and, if you're lucky, there is one incorrect answer that can be disregarded as a possibility. Content mastery will only get you so far on an AP exam. There's another factor at play. Gut instinct. Raw intuition. The ability to *feel* the right answer choice, not just know it. Therapist Patricia Bear, says, "We live in a culture that overvalues intellect. If you say about a person, 'She is so thoughtful,' that is a compliment. If you say, 'She is so emotional,' that is not a compliment. The focus and attention on giftedness then eclipses other activities and interests and prevents gifted children from getting inside their bodies and emotions."

Current curriculum in many schools requires students to justify their answers. They not only have to know the correct answer, but also use critical thinking skills to explain why that answer is the best answer. On the surface, this seems like a good idea, doesn't it? If you don't know why something was the right answer, you may not be able to reproduce those results again because you may have chosen the right answer for the wrong reason. While it is fine to ask students to justify answers sometimes, when we do it all of the time, we decrease their ability to rely upon their intuition.

This is often due to a misunderstanding of what intuition really is. In a recent casual conversation, a therapist friend mentioned that there are only two things humans are naturally afraid of: heights and snakes. We don't have to be taught to fear those things. Everything else is a learned fear. Yet fear feels instinctual, doesn't it? Intuition is a complex interplay between experience and learning and the brain's manipulation of that experience. Intuition, therefore, is far closer to critical thinking than it is to pure emotion. We must have critical thinking for intuition to occur.

Understanding the relationship between intuition and critical thinking has the power to influence more than marking the *best* right answer on a test. When we continually ask people to justify their reasoning, we may subvert their ability to believe in their own choices—and unwittingly nurture unhelpful perfectionism as we enhance their self-doubt. One reason eyewitness accounts are often flawed is that as we talk about events, we often unintentionally change our memory of them. This phenomenon, known as "verbal overshadowing," can also lead students to allow themselves to be talked out of even correct answers when challenged to provide a rationale for the choice. To avoid this, we should make sure on occasion that we allow others to simply state their impressions, their answers, and their responses without defense. It can be helpful to say things like, "Is that what your gut is telling you?" or "Maybe you should go with your intuition on that one." As we allow youth to feel as though we value their instinct, they develop self-confidence, a key factor in self-concept.

Adding it All Up

While many factors affect a person's susceptibility to perfectionism, one commonality is a lack of effective self-concept. As a child learns and implements strategies to develop a healthy self-concept based on reasonable expectations and accomplishments, the pressure to be perfect diminishes. Self-concept development is particularly useful to address self-oriented perfectionism and to avoid self-harm. By working with children to develop realistic expectations of themselves and developing their belief in their ability to *do* things, not just *be* things, we create the kind of self-concept that piles the poker chips in front of them. They will take thoughtful risks, both personal and academic, that lead to real growth. They move away from an attempt to be perfect and toward an attempt to grow.

Key Ideas

- ◉ Poor self-image, even at very young ages, can feed perfectionism.
- ◉ Societal pressures affect both boys and girls, and both the fashion and media industries are common sources of pressure.
- ◉ Developing an inherent sense of self-worth is one key to developing a strong and effective self-concept. Service to others is one way to develop a strong sense of self-worth.
- ◉ Awareness of one's strengths and accomplishments builds self-concept more effectively than awareness of appearance.
- ◉ Connecting with others in healthy relationships builds self-concept
- ◉ A realistic view of the role of practice and effort in achievement can reduce negative aspects of perfectionism.
- ◉ Allowing intuition without requiring justification can build confidence.

Action Steps

- Incorporate service into your daily lives, teaching children to demonstrate small acts of kindness.
- Consider participating in, or even organizing, larger service projects.
- With your child, start a Pride Line. Consider doing one as a family, recording the small achievements of the members of the family in a non-competitive way.
- Display success symbols as reminders of meaningful achievements.
- Facilitate connecting with others. Help youth find, develop, and maintain quality friendships, not bound by age-group peers.
- Work with children to create opportunities for deliberate practice by doing the following:
- Set a goal for the practice. Rather than say, "Practice for thirty minutes," instead set a small, achievable performance goal such as, "Practice until you can play three measures from memory."
- Share feedback. Parents should take the time to learn enough about the activity in which the child is participating to give some meaningful feedback.
- Encourage the practice of the same task to mastery. Identify critical micro-skills in the domain and practice those.
- Help design a "game day" for schoolwork or other activity that does not already have a built-in game day.
- Increase the use of phrases that encourage kids to trust their gut instinct. Avoid verbal overshadowing by not demanding rationale for all choices.

Living in the Moment Imperfectly

CHAPTER VI

Be wise enough not to be reckless, but brave enough to take great risks.

- FRANK WARREN

In the 1993 movie classic *Groundhog Day*, comedian Bill Murray plays an arrogant weatherman from Pittsburgh named Phil Connors, who is sent to Punxsutawney, Pennsylvania, by his TV station to cover the sighting (or not sighting) of the groundhog who will predict six more weeks of winter if he sees his shadow, or an early arrival of spring. Phil is not impressed with this assignment, considering it beneath him. The morning of February 2nd, Groundhog Day, he wakes up to the radio playing Cher's "I Got You Babe." It's more than a song—it's a message. Phil is trapped in time, repeating February 2nd over and over again, waking each morning to the same song, the same day, the same town, and the same events. For days on end, he relives February 2nd until finally he has a change of heart, and after he morphs from the arrogant, narcissistic jerk he was at the beginning of the movie into a kind, compassionate man who looks out for others and genuinely cares for them, he is able to move on. He wakes up to the same song, but it's finally February 3rd, and he can go forward with his life.

Many people struggling with perfectionism create a Groundhog Day experience for themselves, fixated on redoing the same thing over and over again, trying to get it right. They don't move forward; they don't move on. In the end, it ruins the joy they could have felt in imperfect results. Of course, it's not a perfect analogy because Phil Connors really did need to change, and he ended up a better person at the end. Perfectionistic people tend to focus on their faults and imperfections, even if they are small.

Don't Postpone Joy

Even if we wanted to, living the same day over and over until we get it right isn't an option. We can't relive the same day over and over again. We only have *this* day, and we need to live it. Tomorrow will be different.

One September morning when I was home from work, a friend called me urgently saying, "Turn on your TV," and hung up. Clicking the remote, I saw the second plane fly into the World Trade Center. Unable to process what I was seeing at first, I walked toward the television in shock, tripping because I was so focused. I found out later that I had broken my toe, even though I felt no pain in the moment because I knew one huge thing: the world was about to change. Because I had been an intelligence analyst in the Army, I look at events a little differently. I could see security changes coming, and they did; yet something else happened, too. People began to see each other differently. Families grew closer. People were nicer to each other. People said, "I love you" to family members more often. Bumper stickers sprouted up, advising, "Don't postpone joy!"

This is excellent advice that sends a particularly important message to those struggling with perfectionism because perfectionism is, at its heart, the postponement of joy. It postpones joy you could have had in the moment because you are focused on lack, rather than on plenty. It's a scarcity mentality that says, "If I can't have it the way I want it, it's the same as having nothing." A powerful antidote to perfectionism is to truly grasp the truth that living in the present is the only reasonable place to be. Instead, perfectionists more often focus on the past and the future. They agonize over past failures and worry about future possibilities, while the present passes them by, unnoticed and undervalued. If they *are* in the "now," it is a time of anxiety and discomfort for them.

As adults, we must help kids understand that today is special because we're living it. I'm writing this on a bright, sunny Monday morning. Part of my enjoyment of this day will depend upon my understanding its value, yet without becoming paralyzed by its importance. This will be the only chance I have to live this one day. Mondays are special. They are a fresh start. The whole week stretches before us on Mondays. Anything feels possible on Monday. I'm not going to worry about doing everything perfectly today, and I'm not going to live this Monday as if it were Tuesday, thinking all day about what it is I'm going to do tomorrow. I'm going to live today as today. We can vocalize these truths when talking with children, and avoid always discussing or focusing on what's coming in the future, while sometimes failing to help them live in happiness available to them right now.

Shifting Our Motivation Strategy

It is easy to inadvertently communicate to high ability individuals that the only reason to live today is to benefit us on some future day. We talk about getting good grades so kids can get into a good college, and we try to motivate our children and students with promises (or threats) of future reward or punishment. I know you want the best future for your child, but threat reasoning or distant promises are mistakes on several levels.

First, just look at the practical side. If a child is eight years old, and a teacher is trying to motivate him by talking about a test he will take at the end of the school year, that is a very long way off to a child—too far, in fact, to be useful as a motivator. Trying to get a child to complete a homework assignment in September under threat of failing a test in May is ineffective. It's an enormous expanse of time to a child who counts down to exciting events by tracking how many "sleeps" it is. Likewise, imagine that you were really unhappy at work, and a co-worker said, "Oh, don't worry. Your boss is going to retire in ten years." Would that comfort you? Unlikely. The timeline is so far out as to be meaningful. While to adults, nine months is just around the corner, to a child it is a large percentage of his or her life.

Another reason for the lack of effectiveness of this strategy is that it flies in the face of mentally healthy living. Earlier, we discussed how goals exist to give us the journey. Focusing exclusively on an event in the future or using it to justify misery in the moment, can ruin the journey and put too much pressure on the goal. I'm *not* suggesting that sacrifice, hard work, and even a little misery are never a good idea. My youngest son, Joseph, described a movie he'd just seen about Símon Bolivar, the Venezuelan soldier and revolutionary—"Mom, in the movie it really shows how nothing worth having comes without great sacrifice." As a pre-law Latin American Studies major, Joseph is himself making tremendous sacrifices and working very hard to pay his way through college with an Army ROTC scholarship. He is often tired, cold, and suffering physical pain, but loves every minute of it. A key difference in one's ability to tolerate an unpleasant journey is whose goal it is. Sometimes, we use threat-reasoning with things that are not the child's goal, but rather a goal imposed by others, and that is the path to misery for all parties.

If there are behaviors adults know are desirable for children, but are less desirable from the child's perspective, adults can influence that perception. Spoiler: it's not through threats. In a study[42] at Cornell University's Food and Brand lab, 186 four-years-olds who were given veggies with cool names like "X-ray Vision Carrots" and "Power Peas" ate nearly twice as much of those healthy foods as when they were labeled simply "carrots" or "peas." Even after the cool name labels were removed, the kids continued to eat more of those foods. It turns out that kids will eat more broccoli if we call it "dinosaur trees." It's a matter of re-framing the task.

This technique works with older children and teens, as well. In my classroom, homework tasks are called "Extended Learning Opportunities" or ELO, and often accompanied by a snippet of Electric Light Orchestra music (particularly the song with the lyric, "Don't bring me down!"). Tests are "Knowledge Demonstrations." Basic chores in our house were called "Citizen of the Household" rather than chores. Of course, we all know what the things actually are, yet there is power in positive nomenclature, even when it's not a mystery.

We can influence attitudes towards tasks by changing the way we label and treat them. Too often, we make the most important behaviors the least pleasurable. Our own attitudes towards these things are negative, making the situation much worse and running counter to all we know of human motivation.

Waking Up from the Homework Nightmare

When I met twelve-year-old Dominique, her mother was so frustrated with what she called the "homework nightmare" that she was considering sending Dominique to live with her father and step-mother for a school year. Dominique's perfectionism was making homework a brutal experience for everyone, made more difficult by the fact that, on the surface, it wasn't obvious that it was perfectionism. "I know it sounds horrible," she told me, "but sometimes I just want to smack her. She's sitting at the kitchen table throwing these enormous fits, and it's all I can do not to belt her across the head. I'm so scared I'll actually do it one day, and I'm so frustrated with both of us." As I talked with Dominique's mom, I asked her to describe the afternoon routine.

As in many families, the routine was for Dominique to come home from school, have a snack, and then do homework. After her homework was done, she was allowed to play until dinner. This last part was theoretical only, as Dominique never actually completed her homework. No matter how simple the assignment, Dominique somehow tried to turn it into a doctoral dissertation. I asked Dominique's mom to take a video for me of Dominique doing a single math problem. In the video, it looked like Dominique could stretch a math problem like it was made of saltwater taffy. A single, fairly simple problem took her over twenty minutes, and was interrupted by three trips to the bathroom, a break to pet the cat, four trips to sharpen a pencil, and one skirmish with her little brother. I was exhausted just watching it. Sound familiar to anyone?

To start with, I wanted to know if Dominique had any issues that might be influencing this behavior that were beyond my expertise. Did she have mental or physical health issues that would make this scenario more probable? The answer was no. The family had her evaluated the year before by a well-regarded counselor. Dominique was visiting the counselor regularly, but in a family counseling situation to help the children adjust to the parents' divorce, not for her own mental health. If that is not the issue, then we need to look at the environment. Parents, don't get itchy. I'm not blaming you. I am saying that sometimes we inadvertently undermine ourselves by setting up processes that work against us, rather than for us.

Although we can debate the benefits of homework, individual parents can't control it, unless they're homeschooling, so we must focus on making it work for the child. Dominique's mom emailed all of the teachers who assigned homework, explained that she was working to improve

Dominique's feelings about homework, and asked them to share with her the purpose of homework in their classes. The math teacher said it was practice. The language arts teacher said it was reading or writing for longer periods than the school day allowed for.

After a lot of conversation, and a little trial and error, here is what worked with Dominique. First, we changed the structure of the afternoon. By having her do her homework before anything else, we were sending a message that it was an undesirable chore to be endured before fun stuff could be done. The new structure had Dominique come home, eat a quality snack, and then engage in some gross-motor activity for about twenty minutes. Dominique loves to dance, so her mom subscribed to an internet-based on-demand dance class (it cost about fifteen dollars a month) that Dominique could do every day. Her mother began calling homework "extended learning opportunity" or "ELO," as I do in my classroom. I also suggested using different names for classes, making it feel a little more like Hogwarts. Math became "numeracy," science became "potions," and so on.

After that, Dominique sat with her mom for "The Executive Committee." Together, they looked at what homework Dominique had, not just for that day, but also upcoming projects. They discussed the purpose of the assignments, not just what they were, but how they would be useful to her. Using a dry erase calendar with colored markers for different subjects, they planned what would be done when, and how much time each task should reasonably take. Dominique made the time estimates, with mom giving a "confidence interval" rating of how close she thought Dominique would come to that goal. Once the planning was done, which sometimes took five minutes and sometimes took twenty minutes, Dominique would do one small chore that lasted five minutes or less. Once the chore was done, Dominique did twenty minutes of homework, no more, while her mother took her little brother into another room to play.

Before this schedule change, a few helpful bits of information had come out in the discussion. Dominique stated that she loved glitter pens, and she wanted to write with them. Because the teacher didn't allow that, Dominique used glitter pens for practice and regular pen or pencil for assignments being turned in. (Note: it's reasonable for teachers to request certain writing instruments. Some smear, and some are very difficult to read, especially when you are reading tremendous quantities of work.) After twenty minutes, Dominique's mom would come back into the room, and Dominique would take another break, this time a little bit longer one—about ten minutes, usually with her mom. Sometimes they danced around, sometimes Dominique helped prepare dinner, and sometimes she played with her cat. After the second break, Dominique would return to doing homework for another twenty minutes. Then, she would break until after dinner. If there was more homework to complete, it would be done after dinner, with breaks every twenty minutes, for a maximum time spent of an hour and a half each night. Twice a week the schedule was adjusted for church activities and soccer practice.

One key to Dominique's success was that her father and step-mother followed the same plan when she was at their house. Another was open communication with the teachers. Dominique's mom told them about the struggles she was having, and she asked them to share with Dominique how long they thought the homework should take. The hardest thing was negotiating the total homework time. It is not reasonable for children to spend hours each night on homework. The work of children is play, and their brains must have unstructured time to play if they are to grow optimally. At first, Dominique wouldn't complete the homework during the time allotted. I told her mom to let it go, even if it meant her grades suffered, because we were resetting unhealthy habits. Her mom was not to argue or even check her work unless asked by Dominique.

After five weeks, Dominique and her mom sat down for an extended Executive Committee while someone else watched the younger brother. They discussed what was working, and what wasn't, and made some adjustments. There were struggles. Dominique didn't always want to follow the schedule, didn't always want to do what needed to be done. I helped Dominique's mom understand that adults are the same way. We often don't want to do what we should do. Lots of times I've redecorated bulletin boards or talked with other teachers when I should have been grading papers! I told her to resist punishing the behavior. Instead, I suggested she allow Dominique to experience the natural consequences of not completing her homework. By the end of five weeks, while not without problems, the situation was very different from the way it had been. The big power struggles were gone, and every day was no longer a battle.

One issue Dominique had was that her own perfectionism kept her from wanting to complete the homework. She worried she wouldn't do it well enough. When she took the time to look at the rationale and plan the time she would spend, her focus shifted. Interestingly, Dominique's mother became aware of her own perfectionism. She realized that *she* was overly concerned about how other parents or the teacher would judge *her* if Dominique didn't have her homework done. She wanted to be perceived as a good, conscientious mom. We all feel that way sometimes, don't we?

The secret is that even great parents struggle while raising kids. Children are their own people, and not always under as much of our control as we might wish. Yes, Dominique's mom could have taken away privileges or grounded her from other activities—both consequences that are reasonable in other situations—but that would have sent the message that homework was undesirable, and we were specifically trying to change that attitude. It was a shift in thinking we were aiming for, not simple compliance. While every situation is different, Dominique's case demonstrates that sometimes the issues are less about what we're doing, than about the how and the why.

The Importance of Rationale

Asking kids to do things simply to avoid future catastrophic results doesn't work well as a strategy is because it assumes the child places the same value on the future result as the adult does. When we say things like, "Don't you want to grow up to be big and healthy?" to get kids to eat nutritiously, or "I'd hate to see you not be able to take the AP class because you didn't do well in pre-AP," we're assuming that the child cares about the result in the same way we do. Frankly, many kids don't care about growing up healthy. Some perfectionists are secretly hoping they *won't* be able to take the AP class, knowing they'd easily get a 100 on their report card in the regular, on-level class.

Adults are most effective when they help the child see the value in the activity in the moment. How is this helping them now? It may be as simple as asking, "How do you think you'll feel when you show up at school tomorrow with this done?" or "What was it like when Jonas wanted to come over, and you knew he could because all your chores were done?"

Helping children find contemporary value in their work applies to more than school. We need to do the same with everything from cleaning the house to visiting distant family. In our family, we called certain tasks "Citizen of the Household" tasks. They were not tied to allowance or any other value other than good citizenship. They included making your bed, clearing your things out of the car, keeping your dresser drawers straight, clearing your own plate from the dinner table, and putting your clothes in the hamper (until you were old enough to wash them yourself). We decided as a family that it was more pleasant to live in an orderly home.

Of course, this interested me far more than it did my sons. One of my son's, frustrated at not being able to find something one day, said, "That's the problem with a clean house: when you lose something, there's nowhere to look!" They may not have been as concerned as I was with keeping the house orderly, but they all understood that it wasn't fun to eat at someone else's house when you were worried about whether you were eating off of clean dishes. Was our house always perfectly neat? Of course not. It was not the Museum of the American Family. Our home was neat and clean, though, in a way that made it possible for our kids to invite friends over without warning, something that was important to them. Adults must help youth discover inherent values in tasks that appear less-than-ideal on the surface. As we find values in tasks other than achieving scores and stickers, this will not only mitigate perfectionism, but will also set us up for a lifetime of possessing the desirable quality of intrinsic motivation.

We get into trouble when we set goals in far-off time frames partly because youth can't really imagine growing up at all. When I was a child, I saw a movie called *Logan's Run*. In this dystopian film, the society controlled population growth by killing everyone who turned thirty. I remember watching it thinking, "Who'd want to live to be older than thirty? That's old!" If a child wants to set long-term goals for him or herself, that's terrific. In fact, it's ideal. However, long-term goals set by others generally hinder more than help, and can actually diminish children's desire to set their own goals.

The Power of Other

A hallmark trait of gifted children is an earlier-than-typical awareness of the thoughts, feelings, and needs of those around them. This can be powerful in motivating youth. Sometimes, kids who wouldn't do something to benefit themselves will be willing to do it to help someone else. This is, of course, true of adults as well. If we have a child or student who isn't finding any personal benefit in necessary chores, tasks, or assignments, we can help them find motivation in helping others.

My friend Tara has a disabled son named Christopher. Due to brain injury as an infant, he has severe brain damage and cerebral palsy, is confined to a wheelchair, and cannot even roll around on his own. The family needed a new, specially equipped handicap van, which is expensive and not covered by insurance, but they simply could not afford one. A group of friends got together to raise money to help with the down payment. I found myself motivated and energized by this, and decided to donate a portion of my speaking fees to the cause. Every day, no matter how tired I was, I gained strength, energy, and encouragement from knowing I was helping Tara and Christopher. I also learned the "power of other."

When I taught third grade, I would let students pick a charity of the month. Every math problem they did earned a penny's donation to their charity cause. The same kids who would whine about the practice any other time would beg for extra practice sheets to raise money. We made a quilt for a teacher whose husband had died, and I had boys and girls asking to stay in from recess to cut fabric squares. If you have a child resistant to work, consider saying that for every minute of effective work, a benefit will ensue to something or someone else the child cares about, whether a charity, an individual, or a group. The possibilities are broad; it doesn't have to be a monetary benefit.

This moral concern can be used in a different way as well. If a child is resistant to completing work, one useful exercise is for the teacher to explain what happens on his or her part when work isn't done. Typically, as hard as it is to find time to grade papers, it actually takes more time when a student *doesn't* turn in work because you have to contact parents, track the assignment, and then grade it on a deadline at the end of a grading period when the student finally turns it in. If the child has a good relationship with the teacher, it may be effective. At least, a robust discussion of how one's behavior has a ripple effect (the no-man-is-an-island concept), can be a powerful reminder that my behavior affects more people than just me.

Mind in Boat

I recently read Daniel Brown's *The Boys in the Boat*, a story of the University of Washington crew team of 1936. In this powerful, moving story, punctuated by philosophical insights, George Pocock, an artisan boat maker, explains the necessity for oarsmen to keep their minds in the boat while they race, rather than on school, girls, other teams, or anything else. We learn about the role of the coxswain, the small, light person at the back of the boat who calls orders, encouragement, and instruction to the rowers. The coxswain in the story, Bobby Moch, calls out "MIB!" as they row—mind in boat.

The non-oarsman equivalent of mind in boat is mindfulness—paying attention on purpose without distracting thoughts. If the oarsmen focus on the pain of rowing (and it can be agonizing), they lose their rhythm. In the same way, if we evaluate and judge our moments in real time, we lose our rhythm.

Mindfulness arose from the Buddhist tradition, yet it has migrated out of religious practice and into an effective everyday mental practice. In mindfulness, you are fully present in the moment, aware of how you are feeling, what you are sensing. "You then transfer this to your interactions with others," says Patti Bear (whom you met in Chapter 1). In your mindfulness, you think, "How am I reacting to this, where is it coming from, and should I share that reaction with others?"

Mindfulness is the ultimate living in the moment skill, and it has the potential to be very effective against perfectionism. If I can be truly mindful in the moment of the work I'm doing, I am not going to be focused on the score it will earn in the future or how I might fall short, but rather in the full experience now. In my classes, I sometimes gently say "MIB" to help my students remember the need to focus on mindfulness.

As Dan Peters writes in his book, *Make Your Worrier a Warrior,* "Of course, staying in the present is easier said than done." He describes the goal as being "to realize that all worrisome problems reside in the future, a time that has yet to exist. Thus, we can use our great thinking brains to solve any problem that occurs in the present, as opposed to worrying about every single problem before it actually happens in the future."[43] Dr. Peters' suggestion works as well for perfectionism as it does for anxiety. Reminding ourselves that it's a goal, rather than something we are either "good" or "bad" at helps us develop our skills at staying focused on the present.

To help kids stay fully present, consider making the environment a pleasant place to be. Good smells, sounds, and atmosphere make a difference. We often underestimate the detrimental effect of distraction on the ability of our kids to think and work, so we must be careful that we are not undermining our own efforts by checking back too often with our kids while they are working. Like checking a cake in the oven too early, it can make even strong efforts collapse.

Mindfulness Exercises

Mindfulness is not only helpful, it is also doable, with a wide variety of resources available for free or very little cost, and these exercises help reduce the tension and anxiety that so often accompany perfectionism and interfere with learning to manage it. Anyone can begin with some simple exercises that are appropriate for children. You can try these together, or you can guide the child in the exercise. They can be done in small bites of time, and they make a terrific way to handle waiting time.

Belly breathing: Sit or lie in a comfortable position. Place your hand on your stomach, between your ribs and your belly button. With each inhale feel your hand move outward from your spine, indicating that your diaphragm is lowering and pulling air all the way to the bottom of your lungs while pushing out the organs in your abdomen. As you exhale notice your hand moving back toward your spine. Focus on each inhale and exhale. As other thoughts come to mind, gently let them go without judgment, and return your focus to your breath.

Counting the breaths: Begin with belly breathing. As you inhale think, *inhale one,* and as you exhale think, *exhale one.* Continue with the next breath and think, *inhale two,* and then *exhale two.* Continue for five breaths to begin with, and work your way up to ten breaths. If you lose count of your breaths, don't judge yourself; simply start over at one.

Stimulating breath: Place the tip of your tongue on the soft tissue just above your upper teeth and keep it there. Breathe rapidly in and out through our nose with your mouth closed. Inhalations and exhalations should be equal and short, and you will feel the muscles in our neck and stomach working hard. Breathe as rapidly as you can and so quickly that you can hear your breath. Start with only fifteen seconds, and gradually add time as you are comfortable. This exercise is energizing rather than relaxing.

Expansive breath: Stand with your feet about shoulder-width apart and your arms straight out in front of you with your hands touching each other and your shoulders relaxed. Inhale and exhale through your mouth for this exercise. As you inhale, spread your hands open and open your arms wide, bring your hands behind you as far as you can, and point your fingertips behind you. Tip your head back slightly and look upward. As you exhale, bring your arms into your stomach and bend over slightly, letting your head hang and looking at your hands. Repeat several times at a comfortable pace.

Power breathing: Stand with your feet about shoulder width apart and your arms hanging comfortably at your sides. Hold your head erect with your chin slightly forward. Imagine that you are standing on a color that represents power, and imagine that you are breathing in a color that represents strength. Follow your breathing for several breaths or minutes, imagining the power and strength flowing into your body with each breath.

Countdown in the sand: Imagine yourself sitting or lying on the beach in the sand. With your non-writing hand, smooth a small area of sand in front of you. With your writing hand write the number 10 in the sand. With your non-writing hand, smooth the sand over, and with your writing hand write the number 9. Continue smoothing the sand over and writing numbers in reverse order until you reach 0. Vary the exercise by starting with any number you wish.

Under the waves: Imagine that you are a pebble that has been dropped in the ocean. The waves may be stormy or calm on the surface of the ocean, and you pass through them. As you sink lower and lower, you notice that the water becomes calmer and more and more still. Look up and notice the waves and weather on the surface of the ocean, while remaining in the calm and still place deeper down in the water.

Muscle tension release: Close your eyes and let yourself be aware or sensations (heat, cool, tingling, heavy, etc.) in one of your hands, and the more you focus on that hand, the more relaxed it will become. Then let the sensation begin to move up your arm toward your shoulder. Repeat this with your other hand, letting it also move up toward your shoulder. Then do the same with each foot, one at a time. Now relax the muscles of your face and your scalp, and become aware of your relaxed breathing and clear mind.[44]

Alice in Repeatland

When I read Lewis Carroll's *Alice in Wonderland* to my young sons, they were quite confused by the Mad Hatter's tea party. As you may remember, the Mad Hatter had irritated the Queen of Hearts. To punish him, she made it six o'clock all the time for him, which in England is teatime. At the Mad Hatter's house, there were biscuits (cookies), cakes, and tea all of the time. My children could not understand how this could not be fantastic. How could you not want to eat like that all of the time? Over the years, they realized you can indeed get sick of repeating an experience, even if they are the most wonderful treats.

If this is true for cake and cookies, it is even more true of schoolwork or other similar tasks, whether pleasant ones or not. Think back to *Groundhog Day*. Many of our perfectionistic students turn assignments into a *Groundhog Day* experience. They repeat the task over and over in a fruitless search for the perfectly done project or essay or brochure or collage or math facts practice—the elusive homework Holy Grail. These are Adelson and Wilson's Aggravated Accuracy Assessors in action.

Linda Kapfer, an educator in the Midwest, coined this phrase: Work is never done. It's just due. Just do it." Work is rarely ever done, in any domain. Clothes find their way to just-emptied hampers. Dishes find their way to just-cleaned kitchen counters. Work is placed in recently-finished turn-in baskets. Even with discrete tasks that are one-and-done, many of us anguish over them, think of how we wish we could do things over, and try to make them better and better to come closer and closer to perfect. But the fact is, work isn't done, it's just due. So we just do it. This is part of learning to live imperfectly in the present.

Avoid Eeyore Thinking

The sad donkey Eeyore is rarely the favorite character from A.A. Milne's *Winnie-the-Pooh* stories, and I would argue it is because Eeyore doesn't know how to live in the moment. Once, when Owl told Eeyore that Christopher Robin was giving a party, Eeyore's response was, "I suppose they will be sending me down the odd bits which got trodden on. Kind and thoughtful. Not at all, don't mention it." Eeyore imagines the worst way it could end, and focuses on that—a mindset common to perfectionists.

We want to ensure that we avoid thinking like Eeyore, who walks around with a cloud over his head all the time. Everyone is not against us. Everything is not going badly. We will not always get an empty honey pot for our birthday present. Eeyore is a catastrophizer. He looks at every situation from the point of view of how badly it could go, rather than the possibilities in it. Clearly perfectionistic, he does not keep his mind in the boat.

Of course, you can't just snap your fingers and magically get out of Eeyore thinking. I once read that music can shift your mood, but you should do it gradually, starting with songs that echo your feelings, and then adjusting the playlist more towards the mood you want. The idea is to incrementally move the mood, rather than try to do a seismic shift. This makes sense when we are using discussion to encourage youth out of depressing Eeyore-type behaviors. If we tell kids who feel followed by a little grey cloud that everything's fine and they're being ridiculous, and point out all of the ways they are lucky and blessed, we can easily entrench them in a rather sad and gloomy place, because we are telling them they have no right to their feelings. We turn encouragement into an invitation to opposition, which would harm our relationship. Try using the advice regarding music and move the child slowly, buoying them with non-confrontational suggestions and affirmations. Living like Eeyore is not only unhealthy for the child, it is also exhausting for those nearby. Avoid letting mental exhaustion move you towards an ineffective intervention. Be patient. If you find that a child is lingering for long periods of time in the grey and gloom, the issue may be larger than perfectionistic pessimism.

Just Do It

Once when I took my kids to a pool to swim one Texas summer day, the boys all jumped in as soon as we got there. I, on the other hand, gingerly walked down the steps into the pool, gently tapping my hands on top of the water, as if I could keep it lower by doing so. I was fine until the water got to my abdomen, and then it felt cold. One of my sons swam by, splashing me. I objected, calling out, "Don't splash me! Don't get me wet!" My son stopped swimming, stood where he was, and reminded me incredulously, "You're in a *pool*. It's made of *water*. We're here to *wet*." I knew that, yet I didn't want to get too wet, and least not yet. I was so wrong. Who was having more fun, them or me? We have to learn to jump in. We can't linger in the shallow end forever if we are going to live fully. You will have more fun, even if you don't swim perfectly, yet perfectionists tend to be risk-avoiders.

At a Portland, Oregon, advertising company meeting in 1988, company founder Dan Wieden coined the slogan "Just Do It" for the agency's largest client, Nike. This slogan is good advice for those of us who languish in the shallow end, hiding on the steps, desperate not to get wet in the pool of life. Since perfectionists are reluctant to take risks, how do we inspire reluctant youth to "just do it?" Partly, we do so by example. We have to model risk-taking ourselves. We also have to make sure they understand that we will not let them drown, though we may let them struggle a little. And we have to be willing to get in the pool with them. My mother returned to college when I was a teenager, working all day and going to school at night. When I returned to graduate school as a teacher with three young children at home, I remembered her example and was willing to take the risk.

This is especially important with gifted youth because their many abilities make it more likely that they will have to take risks to reach their full potential in any given domain. They will need to try things that few others have done, and risk failure without losing faith in their ultimate success. Whatever our role with children, we must be willing to live our own lives imperfectly in the moment if we want to send that message effectively and persuasively to youth.

Key Ideas:

- We must avoid becoming obsessed with doing things over and over until we get them done perfectly.
- Attempting to motivate youth with far-off promises or threats is ineffective.
- Multiple strategies may be needed to help perfectionistic children develop a healthy relationship with homework.
- It is important to help youth understand the rationale of the work they are doing.
- Often, youth can be motivated by how their actions benefit others as easily or even more easily than they can be motivated to do things for their own benefit.
- Mindfulness training helps young people stay fully present in the moment, a skill that counteracts perfectionism.
- Avoiding Eeyore-like behavior decreases the risk-avoidance and negative self-talk that is common in perfectionistic people.
- Youth who struggle with perfectionism can be influenced to take appropriate risks through effective encouragement and example.

Action Steps

- ⊙ Model the "Don't Postpone Joy" mindset by being open about the joys to be found in daily life. Avoid counting down to weekends or complaining frequently about long days and numerous tasks. Share the successes of the day as well. One suggestion is to have a "one good thing" conversation at dinner, where each family member shares one good thing that happened that day.

- ⊙ Meaningfully motivate youth with strategies more effective than threats or long-term promises. Help them find contemporary meaning in tasks that lie before them. Are they learning a new skill? Are they learning something they could use somewhere else? Are they developing patience? Perseverance? Thoughtfulness? Do they have a feeling of accomplishment when each action is done?

- ⊙ Use the power of their early moral concern to motivate them. Are they helping the family have more harmony by doing their work without complaint? Are they helping the teacher by getting work in on time? Consider setting up a system where their work benefits others, either in a donation or in some other way.

- ⊙ Practice Mindfulness exercises. Consider reading a book on Mindfulness. From time to time, talk about your own Mindfulness.

- ⊙ Gently lure perfectionists out of Eeyore-like thinking with small, optimistic steps. Consider sharing stories of people who, in difficult circumstances, found happiness. Point these stories out in the news or in books you are reading. If pessimistic or depressed behavior persists or is interfering with the normal functioning of the child, seek help.

When Failure Is an Acceptable Option

Failure should be our teacher, not our undertaker. Failure is delay, not defeat. It is a temporary detour, not a dead end. Failure is something we can avoid only by saying nothing, doing nothing, and being nothing.

\- DENIS WAITLEY

About ten years ago, the school district in which I was teaching got a new superintendent. His overarching attitude was embodied in a book he required every teacher to read called *Failure Is Not an Option*. I agree that global failure is not acceptable, and we don't want kids failing entire classes, entire grades, or dropping out of school. However, I'm convinced that micro-failure in many settings should be acceptable in ways that it is not. Micro-failure is low-stakes failure where nothing permanent is at stake, and which helps people learn from the results of their behaviors. Examples of micro-failure would be grades on individual assignments, not making a team one tried out for, coming in last in a 5k race, having a voice break during a song in a concert, or being criticized in front of peers.

Why Failure is Valuable

In business writing. books and blogs frequently address the advantages of failing and learning to fail. Of course, failure can be taken too far, but developing a comfort with failure can be a healthy way to learn to manage perfectionism. It resembles immunotherapy for allergies when people get shots in order to build up a tolerance to allergens. Small "shots" of failure can have the same effect. Particularly when parents and teachers create environments where failure is part of the art of trying hard things. This should not be *just* the child who fails in frequent, small ways. Adults must model this as well. When things don't go as planned, failure then becomes one part of the process of mastery, of exploration, of inquiry, and of quality attempt, and the experiences can be shared as learning experiences.

In my classroom, I have a poster showing a planet exploding and the words "FAIL FORWARD" below it. Underneath the "FAIL FORWARD" slogan is a quote from the great philosopher Yoda that says, "Lost a planet, Master Obi-Wan has, how embarrassing." When students come to me and say, "I got a fifty-seven on this quiz! My life is over!" I ask, "Have you lost a planet?" They groan, knowing what's coming.

"No," they say, waiting for my predictable reply: "Well, then you are not yet at Jedi level failure, young Padowan."

My goal is to help kids keep their perceived failure in perspective. It is important to understand the world is not catastrophically coming to a grinding halt because you got a bad grade. The world is not going to explode. The planet did not disappear simply because something didn't go right for you. The Empire will not defeat the Republic because you got a "B." As with any strategy in classrooms (and homes!), this one depends upon a safe, respectful relationship. My students would not have responded well to this if they did not know I loved them; they would have instead seen it as sarcasm. Often, the best strategies fall flat without the preparation that is first necessary to lay the social and emotional groundwork.

Keeping one's perspective is key to managing perfectionism. Catastrophizing failure is one of the leading causes of debilitating perfectionism. Non-mocking humor, such as this *Star Wars* allusion, is only one strategy for keeping micro-failure in perspective.

A related approach that is needed is to resist the temptation to over-comfort. If we consistently over-comfort children who are overreacting to small failures, we teach them to gain affection through drama. This not only makes them more likely to overreact to the next failure, but also nurtures the unhelpful habit of "learned helplessness." The flip side of this is that we have to make sure we are giving sufficient attention to avoid the dynamic in which youth (even subconsciously) feel that they have to go to pieces in an extreme manner in order to obtain comfort.

The Power of a Ninety-Nine

In addition to the poster, a classroom and home environment that accepts failure, and avoiding over-comfort, parents and teachers can use other strategies to increase comfort with safe failure. The first of these is to help students understand the power of a ninety-nine. During my undergraduate college work, my major was English, and I loved my 4.0. I mean I loved it! I loved it like it was a pet dog. I carried it with me everywhere. I would log in to my student account just to look at my grade point average; I thought about it all the time. In my very last year, very close to being the number one student at my university's graduating class, I took an American Literature class. On the first day, the professor announced, "I should let you know upfront. I don't give 100s."

Excuse me? Surely I did not hear that correctly. You know what I thought? I thought to myself, "I'm going to *make* him give me a one hundred. I'll be the first one hundred he ever gives." I had no doubt at all that I could make that happen. After all, standards had crumbled before me for years when I worked really, really hard.

On the very first test I did a bang-up job. I knew it was fantastic. This test was a work of art. I turned it in with a heart full of joy and with a little bit of "I told you so" vibe. When I got the test back, guess what grade I earned? A ninety-nine. I did what any self-respecting perfectionist would do: I went to the professor's office hours and said, "Excuse me, but I think there's a mistake. I have a ninety-nine on this test, and I think I really deserved a one hundred."

Bless his patient heart, he went through my test with me and showed me syntactical choices I could have made differently that would have strengthened my argument. He showed me missed allusions I could have made to other works that would have strengthened my examples. I understood, and I was ready for the next test.

When the second test came, I was ready. I could have written the test. What did I earn? A ninety-nine. And where was I? Back at his office hours. This went on all semester: five tests, five ninety-nines. Eventually, it was time for the final exam. He gave us seven possible essay topics, and one would be chosen for the exam. I decided to do what anyone would do: I wrote out and memorized all seven essay choices. Isn't that normal? I was ready to come into class, sit down, and write a perfect essay. There was no way he was not giving a one hundred on that.

On the day of the final, seven beautiful essays in my memory, I brought in a manila envelope, self-addressed and stamped because I knew he was going to mail me the first and only one hundred that he had ever given. I was going to put it up on my refrigerator where it was going to live in perpetuity in a shrine to perfectionism.

When I saw the topic, I rejoiced. I remembered the whole essay. I can still remember the excitement I felt when I turned it in. Perhaps you can see what's coming. When I got it back in the mail, I eagerly tore the envelope open. What score was there in the upper right-hand corner of my paper? A ninety-nine. My fury knew no bounds. I went to his office hours, and I said, "What is going on? This essay was perfect!"

And he changed my life with what he said to me. "Lisa," he said. "I could easily have given you a one hundred at the very beginning of this semester, but your ninety-nines at the end of the semester were so much better than your ninety-nines at the beginning of the semester. And if I had given you a one hundred to start with, you would have had nowhere to grow."

If you get a one hundred right away, you will have nowhere to grow. What we want is not to try for a hundred, but to try for growth. After that experience, I decided that when I became a teacher, I wasn't going to give a one hundred on a subjective grade either. For objective assessments like multiple choice, yes, a one hundred is on the table. It's unfair to say, "Oh, you should have written your name in calligraphy." If, however, it's a subjective assignment, then I'm going to give less than a one hundred because there will always be room for growth. Along with that grade, I'm going to make sure—and this is key—that I share what the room for growth was.

In my experience, many bright students are used to getting perfect scores with little or no feedback. This is not only disheartening, but it also creates a climate in which perfectionism flourishes because if you don't know what you did to earn that high grade, you have to try to get every component exactly right on the next assignment, seeking the perfect score. Less-than-perfect scores, with robust feedback, reduce perfectionism and increase growth. Embrace the power of the ninety-nine.

The Amish Mistake

The next strategy is to use the idea of the Amish mistake. When my sister-in-law was getting married, I decided to learn to quilt so that I could make her a quilt for a wedding present. It turns out that it's much harder to sew a straight line than one would think. As I was learning to quilt, trying to master the art of the straight seam and the perfect corner, I made mistake after mistake after mistake. To be honest, the finished product looked much better if you stepped back a few feet and squinted. My friend, Renée, who was teaching me how to quilt, would say after every mistake, "Oh, that's your Amish mistake."

She told me that there is a belief that the Amish put a mistake in their quilts on purpose so that they are not pretending to be God. They recognize that only God is perfect, and they are not perfect. I would never in all my life have put a mistake on purpose in my quilts because I make plenty mistakes by accident. It turns out that this idea of the Amish Mistake, sometimes called the "Humility Square," is a myth, and if you quilt any amount of time, you will learn there are a lot of quilting myths. When I was speaking in Lancaster, Pennsylvania, I met some Mennonite quilters who confirmed to me that the idea of the Amish mistake is a fallacy. They feel that the myth itself feels like the opposite of humility. They object to the idea that people might think Amish quilters believe that they would make a perfect quilt if not for the intentional error. But I have met quilters who deliberately put in what they call a God square, where they turn a square to be wrong for just that ideal.

Nevertheless, we can still use it as a strategy. We can voice to kids and even ourselves that a mistake simply demonstrates what we already knew— we are not perfect. When we make a mistake, no matter how silly, no matter how simple, we just say, "You know what? That's my Amish mistake." Because no one is perfect.

One psychologist uses a similar strategy with perfectionists. He says he wants the client to be as perfectly human as possible. Since humans are not perfect (only Gods are), he asks the client to do one thing each day imperfectly (on purpose), but to do that thing as "perfectly imperfect" as possible, and then to come back and tell him how it went and how he felt. This kind of "paradoxical instruction" can help perfectionists practice becoming more comfortable with "less than perfect."

Sometimes, our perspectives of what constitutes failure influence perfectionism, not only for ourselves, but also for those around us. When José's mom asked for a conference with his teacher, the teacher was surprised. José was doing well in the class, both socially and academically, and his performance seemed aligned with his ability. During the conference, José's mother explained that she was extremely unhappy with a "B" on the report card José had brought home the week before. He had never received lower than an "A" before. The teacher shared with José's mom what factors contributed to the grade, and explained that although José was working hard, he may not earn an "A" in the future, either.

"But that's like an 'F'," said the mom. "In my world, a 'B' is the same as an 'F.'"

The experience of the teacher and parent demonstrates one of the components of failure: it's relative.

If you look "failure" up in a dictionary, you'll find references to the two components of failure—a lack of success or the omission of expected action. In the story above, it was not a lack of success that the mom considered to be failure, but rather the omission of the expected action of the earning of an "A."

This is the type of failure that is the most common in perfectionists, particularly the gifted. It's the more difficult of the two types to address because what looks like failure to one person, in this case the mother, looks like success to another, in this case the teacher.

Providing Support in Dealing with Failure

When we feel a sense of failure, but others don't see it the same way, we may feel isolated as well as demoralized. We feel our concerns are not taken seriously, that we are treated as we if we are making a mountain out of molehill, or that our disappointment is an over-reaction. When this happens repeatedly, the perfectionist is likely to go underground with the perceived failure, hiding the pain of it, and often becomes more and more reluctant to attempt anything that might result in a similar failure.

On the other side of that equation, one of the most difficult things for adults to do is to really give support when we feel that the child truly is being ridiculous about his or her reaction to what he/she perceives as failure. If it's out of proportion to what really happened, it can be very hard to be supportive. As discussed earlier, there is a fine line between providing support on the one hand and enabling overly dramatic reactions on the other.

So how can we address this effectively and appropriately? First, remember to ask, don't tell. Try to avoid saying, "You shouldn't make such a big deal about this" or "You need to calm down." Instead, ask in a sincere way something like, "Why does this feel so painful to you?" or "What is bothering you the most about this?"

When asking children what they believe is influencing the feelings they have, possible prompts include:

- Were you surprised by this?
- Did you feel embarrassed about this?
- Did you feel pressured to _______ (get a certain grade, etc.)?
- On a scale of one to ten, how upset are you about this right now?
- Do you think you will still be this upset tomorrow?
- Do you feel like you have the power to feel better?

It's important to avoid sounding patronizing or mocking. At the same time, avoid over-sympathizing. It is possible that the answers to these questions may surprise you. At the root of the temper tantrum over something small is often the very deep fear that they are globally inadequate. On the other hand, the size of the reaction doesn't always align with the depth of the feelings. We are all capable of hiding deep feelings or over-reacting to relatively small issues. A lack of sleep, hunger, and other dynamics unrelated to the issue itself can skew the reaction. Asking probing, yet respectful, questions will allow parents to better understand how upset the child actually is and will help the child begin to develop a sense of perspective. This process can take time, as youth learn to better self-reflect about the depth of their feelings. When someone asks them to consider how they're feeling, it forces a pause in their reaction. Over time, this can nurture their ability to better manage those negative feelings.

In addition to asking, as opposed to telling, another way to provide support in dealing with failure is to have a "favorite mistake" board in your house or your classroom to share things that went wrong. In a classroom, you can set aside one bulletin board as the place you can put up lesson plans that go horribly wrong (even though they may have come highly recommended by others). You can share critical email you receive or even negative comments on social media. Students can put up poor quiz grades, terrible tests, and even screenshots of their boyfriend's breaking up with them on Facebook.

It's a great place to make it safe to not be perfect. Be sure also to keep a little pad of sticky notes nearby so students can share how they fixed whatever went wrong for them. Students write things like, "I did test corrections" or "My teacher wrote a different lesson plan" or "I quit that one in the middle of it and went on to something new" or even "I found a new boyfriend." As it becomes a pattern to identify things that went wrong and how they eventually went well or were corrected, youth can begin to look forward to the resolution even in the moment of the perceived failure.

Favorite Mistake Boards aren't just for classrooms. They also work in kitchens! Families can share movies that turned out to be poor choices, recipes that didn't work out, or other times when things did not go as planned. Homes should be perfection-free zones, with parents leading the way. Saying good-bye to our own perfectionism makes it safer for our children to be less than perfect as well.

Practicing the Possibilities

A fuel for perfectionism is that perfectionists live in the land of perfect possibility. They envision the way it could be, and they get very disappointed when it turns out in a way that doesn't match that vision. You may have had the experience of trying to imitate something you found online or in a magazine, only to realize that you cannot make it look like that person did. The feeling is often an awkward mixture of discouragement, disappointment, and frustration. We often compare our worst to others' best—our tryout or dress rehearsal compared to their ready-for-prime-time presentation. We often forget that what we see online is the result of photo manipulation, multiple takes, and professional designers.

Sometimes, with youth, it is helpful to ask them to predict what's going to happen so that they can be more aware of their expectations, fears, and self-talk. We ask three key questions: "What is the absolute best thing that could happen? What's the worst thing that could happen? What's the most likely thing that could happen?" If all we have in our minds is the best possibility, we see anything less than that as failure. If we focus on the worst-case scenario, we can be too discouraged to even begin. Focusing on the most-likely scenario allows for a reset to reasonable expectation. As we practice predicting what's most likely, we back off the perfectionist cliff where we think the only acceptable outcome is the best-case scenario. This is an effective way to avoid the Eeyore-like thinking discussed in Chapter 6. We also sometimes say to them, "What is the evidence for each of the three alternatives?"

In his book *Freeing our Families from Perfectionism,* Tom Greenspon suggests a similar strategy. He says, "Select what seems best, and plan for the consequences of that choice."[45] He describes a common situation in which perfectionists struggle to get started, paralyzed by less-than-desirable possibilities. His idea adds another layer to practicing the possibilities that includes planning, an exercise that is particularly helpful with perfectionistic procrastination.

Barbara Clark's Model

Clark recommends a series of questions to ask a child who is upset. The first question is to simply ask, "What happened?" It's surprising how often what *we* think is upsetting the child is not the root cause at all, but rather some other experience entirely.

The "What happened" question is followed by, "What's the problem?" We've all had the experience of hearing about what happened, yet remaining confused about why that's an issue. Sometimes what would appear to be a most likely concern is not actually the heart of the issue at all. Genuinely asking what the problem is can help you glean critical information.

The next step is to ask, "What are you doing to solve the problem?" Focus on action at this point, not emotion. Don't worry about the feelings yet. Don't ask how they feel. They're too upset to talk about that because the emotions they are experiencing in this moment are really wound up. You're trying to introduce calm, and the time to talk about the feelings is once we've deescalated a little bit. This model effectively forces pragmatism into an emotionally charged situation.

I once served as the expert consultant to the television show *Child Genius*, and we would often see children with incredibly disproportionate reactions to missing a question or two. The temper tantrums would have been more understandable if they had just found out they were moving the next day away from everything they'd ever known, not just missing a single question in a sea of dozens of questions. Sometimes the parents were ineffectual in dealing with these tantrums, and as the consultant, I could only stand by and watch as they often made the situation worse.

Clark's model could have helped many of these children to focus on action. By asking, "What are you doing to solve the problem?" you refocus the child to action, rather than the abyss that is the disappointment or anger. The action doesn't have to be big. It can be something as small as "I'm writing in my journal about it" or "I'm just taking five minutes to cry it out."

The next question to ask is, "Is it working?" If the answer to the question is yes, then allow the child to work through it, even if the child seems very upset. Letting them feel those feelings without interference is fine as long as they feel like what they're doing is going to work for them. Too often, we are unwilling to allow children to feel unhappy, wanting to fix it and have them return to cheerfulness. It can be hard to step back and allow children to be sad for a while. No normal parent wants to see their child hurting, yet sadness, disappointment and frustration are a normal part of life. As children mature, we must allow them to spend increasingly more time dealing with uncomfortable feelings before we intervene, in the same way we eventually move babies into self-soothing. We also must avoid non-verbal signals that we don't have faith in their plan. If they say it's working, let them try to work it out, as long as their plan is safe. We can revisit the question after a period of time if it seems like what they're doing isn't moving them forward.

If, on the other hand, the answer is no, what they're doing is not working, then we follow up with Clark's next question, which is, "What are you willing to do differently?" It's not helpful to tell a child, "You shouldn't be angry" or "That won't work." Put the decision-making burden back on the child by asking them what adjustments they're willing to make.

You might have to keep revisiting this, using slightly different phrasing, until the child finally comes a point where he or she is either ready to come up with his or her own idea of something different to try, or is ready to hear questions such as, "Would you like to hear what others have tried" or "Would you be willing to try something else?" The emphasis here is on the idea that we are *inviting* the child to consider other options, rather than forcing the ideas on the child. Even if the idea you have to share is something you yourself have tried, you may want to phrase it as, "Some people have found that *xyz* worked," rather than, "I always...." Children often express disinterest in solutions that are too parental. I found this to be the case with my own children, who, even though I taught English, didn't necessarily want me writing critiques on their essays.

If you find that a child experiences frequent meltdowns, you might create a poster with a list of possible things to try when feeling angry, frustrated or sad. Possible examples include:

- I will write in my journal (non-writers can use a camera or voice recorder to record feelings).
- I will do fifty jumping jacks (or other gross motor exercises).
- I will breathe deeply ten times.
- I will brush the dog for fifteen minutes.
- I will write a list of twenty things I do well.

- I will draw a picture or color in a coloring book.
- I will sing a song I like along with the video.
- I will call grandma or grandpa.
- I will shoot fifteen free-throws.
- I will blow bubbles.
- I will take a bubble bath.
- I will read my favorite book for thirty minutes.

This list isn't exhaustive, of course; every child will have different things that calm him/her. The idea is that the child now has a list of possibilities at hand to choose from, rather than the parent reeling off a parent-made list. Brainstorm these possibilities with the child during a calm time. There is an old saying, "In the middle of a hurricane is not the time to try to teach navigational skills." This can be a family activity, with everyone making lists of things that soothe them. Gross-motor activities can especially help those of us who have physical manifestations of emotion.

One reason Barbara Clark's model is particularly useful is that tantrums about perceived failure alienates students from their peers. When kids tantrum or over-react to events other students see as silly or unwarranted, it damages relationships with peers who call them "cry-baby" or other unflattering names. Classmates sometimes perceive bright kids' reactions as arrogance, thinking that they are pretending to be upset in order to brag about how smart they are.

I'm not at all saying that children should hide emotion in order to fit in; rather, I'm saying that we may be unaware of the effect that our reactions to failure have on our relationships with others. This is true even of adults. Recently, I was very upset over a situation that had nothing to do with my husband. I was venting to him about it, and he said, with his hands raised defensively in front of him, "I didn't do it!" I knew that, but what I didn't know was how hostile and attacking I seemed to him. Strong emotion can be abrasive to others, even if it's not directed at them. We don't always realize how we come across.

Creating an environment with a healthy attitude towards failure through the implementation of these strategies goes a long way towards helping perfectionists have a more realistic and healthy relationship with failure. Becoming more comfortable with the idea that failure is a natural, and often even desirable, aspect of life helps control the more debilitating aspects of perfectionism. Families with an action plan for how to handle failure can be incubators of reasonable expectations and self-redirection away from over-reaction. Although not every strategy will work in every situation, having a plan for how to deal with the inevitable frustrations empowers both the child and the parent.

The Fitts and Posner Model

Psychologist Paul Fitts was one of many scientists called for duty in World War II. His service as a Lieutenant Colonel in the United States Air Force gave him a very different study environment from the Ohio State University, and the military experience transformed his research. His interest in aviation safety and on human factors of performance led him to study how people learn tasks and learn them well. With Michael Posner, Fitts published *Human Performance*,[46] and it sought to blend hard science into the softer science of psychology. Fitts and Posner argued that you could quantify the ability of humans to perceive, pay attention, reason, and then act. By applying psychology to engineering, it transformed thinking about human performance.

Fitts and Posner described three levels of acquisition of expert performance, particularly in sensorimotor tasks. First, during the Cognitive Phase, the learner acquires an understanding of what he or she is supposed to do. In this phase, you make a lot of errors, and you have no idea of how to fix them. It takes tremendous focus. You're slow. You're bad at it. Many people quit right here, discouraged at slow progress. If you've ever taken piano lessons, you are intimately aware of what this stage feels like. Every note feels overly deliberate. No sound coming from your fingers could be construed as music. It's frustrating.

If you stick with the activity, you will move into the Associative Phase where you become more consistent in your execution. You can pay less attention to make the correct movements. You make fewer errors, and they are less egregious than errors made in the Cognitive Phase. Even more importantly, you become better at figuring out why you made the errors, and you even have an idea of how to correct them. When you do it wrong, you know what went wrong.

People who stick with the activity through the Associative Phase enter the Autonomous Phase stage of performance acquisition. In this final phase, you're on autopilot. You don't have to think about what you're doing—you just do it. In fact, if you think about it, you may do it less well. For example, thinking about typing while you are doing it will slow you down. In *Moonwalking with Einstein*, Josh Foer calls this the "OK Plateau," and this is where most of us throw in the towel on improvement.[47] Once you get here, for the most part you don't get better, or you get better so slowly and incrementally that it's not noticeable.

The key to getting better is to force yourself to stay in the first stage, the Cognitive Phase, or to at least visit it from time to time. You have to practice differently, deliberately pushing yourself into conscious effort by exceeding your skill. People who are fantastic musicians practice like they're bad at it. Instead of playing whole songs, they work on small phrases. Tiger Woods does not practice by going out and playing 18 holes of golf, right? He works on small behaviors. In order to be better, we break the activity apart into little chunks of smaller skills, and we push ourselves past our ability in them to the point of failure over and over again. That's how we get better. Adults must teach this to children or they will quit too often and too early. They become good, but never great, and they blame their perfectionism rather than their decision to stay in the Autonomous Phase.

One Thursday evening, I went to see the Mormon Tabernacle Choir practice and settled myself into a pew, expecting to enjoy an evening of beautiful music. I was so wrong. I never, not once the entire night, heard a song sung through from beginning to end. Instead, I heard bits and pieces of songs. Because they often sang in sections, I only heard the tenor line or only the alto line. While interesting, informative, and useful for understanding how the choir operates, I didn't hear what I had expected.

What the Choir and its director know is that in order to remain the greatest choir in the world, they must stay in the Cognitive Phase. They must think deliberately and intentionally about their music. They cannot simply sing songs over and over and expect to be amazing. They would still be good, but they would not be the best. Too often, gifted children, particularly those who are perfectionistic, feel like they've beaten the game when they reach the Autonomous Phase and they shun practice, saying things like, "I already know that." Ah, but that's not the point, is it? The point is, can you force yourself to behave as if you don't know, force yourself to look at its parts and work on them? If you force yourself to failure, real growth awaits you.

Key Ideas

- Developing a comfort level with non-permanent, low-stakes failure is a key to managing perfectionism.
- Telling people how to feel is far less effective than asking them how they feel with appropriate, open-ended questions.
- Providing the appropriate level of support in the face or real or perceived failure helps students manage perfectionism and also helps them interface more effectively with peers.
- Creating a plan for dealing with failure experiences can help youth manage their emotions related to the failure.
- Returning to the Cognitive Phase of talent development leads us to expert performance.

Action Steps:

- Use the following conversation starters to open a dialogue:
- What were you hoping to earn on that assignment?
- What would it have felt like if you had gotten the grade you wanted?
- Was there anything reasonable you should have done to change the outcome?
- How do you think you'll feel about this in a week? A month? A year?
- Create a "Favorite Mistake" board in your home or classroom.
- Give thorough feedback, not just a grade or a "good job." Always share the elements of the task that contributed to the high achievement.
- Discuss the idea of the "Amish Mistake." Point out the mistakes you make, sharing that these mistakes are simply part of creating.
- Have children keep a journal, recording how they dealt with failure (real or perceived).
- Familiarize yourself with Barbara Clark's model.
- Create a list of techniques to manage negative emotions.
- With the child, consider a task or activity from the Fitts and Posner model, looking at small skills that make up that activity. Try to return to the Cognitive Phase with those skills, setting practice goals that focus on the micro-skill, rather than the entire activity.
- List five things the child is currently learning, either at school or in extra-curricular activities. Rate each one as being in one of the three Fitts and Posner phases. Use the activity as a time to discuss the activity and how the child feels about it.

Building Resilience

Perfectionism is not the same thing as striving to be our best. Perfectionism is not about healthy achievement and growth; it's a shield.

- BRENÉ BROWN

Just days before Alexandra Scott celebrated her first birthday, she was diagnosed with neuroblastoma, a disease that makes up 6% of all childhood cancers. After a stem cell transplant at age four, Alex decided to operate a lemonade stand to raise money to help other children with cancer. The first lemonade stand raised $2,000, but Alex wasn't finished. Until her death at age eight, Alex continued to work to raise money so that others could survive the disease that was taking her life. She set an ambitious goal: she wanted to raise one million dollars. By the time she died, her little lemonade stand had grown, and she met her goal. Since then, the Alex's Lemonade Stand Foundation[48] has raised over 120 million dollars, funding 650 critical research projects at over 100 hospitals and research institutions.

Not every child has the strength and resilience of Alexandra Scott, yet even very young children face threats and challenges to their emotional and physical well-being that make resilience a vital trait for emotional and mental health. The American Psychological Association defines resilience as "the ability to adapt well to adversity, trauma, tragedy, threats or even significant stress[2]." People with perfectionistic tendencies frequently struggle with resilience; the experience discouragement and hopelessness instead. Resilience is essential, and the strategies we use to build it in children help them build strong defenses against the defeatism (I won't even try because I'll probably fail) that so often accompanies perfectionism.

Begin with the Brain

Francis Galton had an idea. It began with the work of his more famous cousin, Charles Darwin, and it took Darwin's work toward a worrisome end. If one considered survival of the fittest and the power of heredity, then it stood to reason that it would benefit all mankind to be more selective in its breeding than it had been through the ages? Galton developed the idea of "eugenics," literally "good birth," and believed strongly that tall men should marry tall women, that smart men should marry smart women, and that those who were feeble minded and otherwise inferior should avoid reproducing at all. Genes, he believed, were everything. Others took his ideas and ran with them, including people like Adolf Hitler, who believed not only in the possibility but also the desirability of building a master race.

Galton's beliefs stood in stark contrast to the ideas of philosopher John Stuart Mill who saw children as a "tabula rasa," or blank slate, and believed that any child could be formed into whatever the parents wished through manipulation of the environment. Would you like to raise a sea captain? Simply fill the child's room with pictures of the ocean and the child's mind with tales of the sea. Would you like to raise an engineer? Then surround the child with designs and puzzles and building toys. For decades, the nature versus nurture argument has raged, with one theory widely accepted at one time, only to be rapidly supplanted by another.

Recently, both theories have given way to the immense and growing research on the brain demonstrating that ability and personality are formed neither by nature nor nurture, but rather a complex interdependence of the two that determines not only physical, but also psychological traits. Explained very simply, this is how it works. At birth, a child has 23,000 genes inherited from parents. This is called the "structural genome." Scientists often liken the structural genome to the hardware of a computer. While any use of a computer as a metaphor for the human brain falls apart quickly, it is useful for understanding the role of the brain in the determination of resilience. If you have a computer with a certain video card, a certain amount of memory, and a certain processor, you know the limits of that computer's capacity.

In addition to hardware, a computer needs an operating system on which to run. The brain has an operating system as well, and this is called the "epigenome." The epigenome determines at what level of capacity the hardware will function, and what parts to use. The epigenome, in effect, "turns on" certain parts of the hardware. Frances Champagne,[49] a professor of psychology at Columbia, uses a library metaphor instead of a computer. She says your genes are like shelves filled with books, and the epigenome determines which books are taken down from the shelves and read. The scientific term for the "reading" of the genes is "expression." When genes are read, or revealed, they are expressed. The study of this phenomenon is called epigenetics.

Current scientific studies reveal that many factors influence the expression of genes. These factors include nutrition or its lack, nurturing or its lack, abuse, neglect, hormones, pesticides, other chemicals, and more. Our bodies are constantly reacting to our environments, both physical and emotional. Studies[50] have shown that when children experience persistent, long-term stress, resilience is often diminished in subsequent years, even into adulthood. The reverse also appears to be true. Children raised in loving homes with supportive families and strong learning environments get the brain's "resiliency book" read and the relevant genes expressed.

As we build resilience in children as a defense against perfectionism (or at least against its negative consequence), we must begin with the architecture of the brain itself. While resilience seems very touchy-feely, residing firmly in the affective domain, in reality it has its roots in our DNA. This is not to say that children who come from troubled homes or who have endured long-term stress cannot be resilient. It does mean that the odds are more against them because of their experiences, and that adults should recognize the environmental impact of both a child's physical and emotional care.

The Importance of Family Mealtimes

Perhaps one of the most efficient and effective places to start improving a child's well-being is the family dinner table, and, no, the minivan filled with fast food does not count. Multiple studies show that the family dinner acts as a type of "vaccine," protecting children against all sorts of ills. Dr. Robin Fox, an anthropologist at Rutgers University, notes that it is not just the sharing of food that makes family dinner so profoundly important. She says, "If it were just about food, we would squirt it into their mouths with a tube. A meal is about civilizing children. It's about teaching them to be a member of their culture."[51] This includes the family culture. As families gather, even families of two, children learn to take turns, to listen, to be listened to, fundamental manners, and other vital skills that help them feel connected to others and enable them to navigate their world outside the home.

A return to the family table gained momentum in 2001 when a study done by the National Center on Addiction and Substance Abuse (CASA) found that teens who eat with their parents do better in school, have less mental stress, and are far less likely to abuse drugs or alcohol. In 2005, CASA[52] released another study showing that families get better at it as they practice, so it is crucial that parents not give up too quickly. One of the most important findings in the study was that kids who ate with their parents were more likely to think their parents were proud of them, a key ingredient in developing confidence in children. As we look at this through the lens of preventing or mitigating perfectionism, these findings are particularly important.

If your family has not yet established a family dinner habit, please begin to do so. Start with one night a week and add on. Consider preparing meals on the weekend for weeknight use. If the time for preparation prevents the holding of family dinner, healthy prepared meals are available. Who cooked the meal is less important than who eats it and with whom. Pediatrician Kenneth Ginsburg wrote, "The stable connection between caring adults and children is the key to the security that allows kids to creatively master challenges and reach their highest potential."[53] That stable connection can be formed and developed around the family table.

DeMarcus and Shonda Johnson remembered the value of family meals from their grandmothers. "Sunday afternoons, we'd all gather at Mama's house," DeMarcus recalls. "I remember enormous platters of food, and I will never forget the day I graduated to the 'grown-up table' from sitting on the floor around the coffee table in the living room with the other children. I wanted that for my own kids." Shonda's memories include listening to the stories of her extended family, and she wanted her children to feel that same sense of belonging she had that came from those shared remembrances. "I felt like a part of something bigger than myself. I had this huge safety net of family, and I was saved from bad decisions more than once by knowing I didn't want to do anything that would be told in hushed tones in my grandmother's kitchen."

The Johnsons decided to commit themselves to dinner as a family. As the children got older and involved in more activities, it became more difficult. They decided that on days when they could not have everyone in the kitchen at the same time at night, they would have breakfast together. Interestingly, it wasn't only their children who benefitted. "When our kids have friends over, they always comment on how much they like having dinner here. So many of them eat in cars or in a rushed, very isolated way. They love being here, and it reminds us why we're committed to this, even though it's hard sometimes."

When Jasmine, their oldest daughter, began to struggle with some perfectionistic behaviors and feelings in high school, the family dinner table was the first line of defense. During that daily time together, they talked openly about what was happening. Shonda found a list of discussion prompts on Pinterest, and they used them to start conversations. "Because we were just drawing the slips of paper from a jar on the table, it wasn't as confrontational as if DeMarcus or I said, 'So, Jasmine, were you a perfectionist today?'" While family dinner together is not a panacea, it is a reasonable, approachable, and effective strategy any family can add to its toolbox.

Family Storytelling

As Shonda Johnson suggested, there is power in the telling of family stories. Recently, the importance of family storytelling has gained traction, and numerous studies have shown its impact on children, specifically with regard to resiliency. Robin Moore, author of *Creating a Family Storytelling Tradition*, says, "Perhaps the greatest benefit of family stories lies in the simple and powerful act of listening. When we feel deeply heard and listened to, it is possible to heal old wounds, build bridges and re-affirm our connections to our family."[54] This kind of listening benefits those struggling with perfectionism, as they find support and acceptance within the framework of the stories and as they hear how others deal with setting goals and trying to achieve them.

In addition to creating closeness and a shared family identity, storytelling traditions introduce and nurture other skills and habits. To tell a story well, one must acquire the ability to use one's voice as an instrument, control the breath, understand the necessity for eye contact, and be deliberate with gestures. Skills like these help children communicate with others, even when others are not necessarily an audience. Children whose parents help them learn to tell others' stories become better tellers of their own stories, facilitating connection with peers, educators, and their parents. Moore says, "True listening begins with the willingness to see the world through another's eyes." These behaviors protect against perfectionism and shield children from its most pernicious effects

At the Emory University Center for Myth and Ritual in American Life (MARIAL), robust research[55] is being done on the power of family narrative, and not just the happy, Pollyanna-like kind, either. To find out how much children knew about their family, the researchers asked them twenty questions, including such questions as:[56]

- Do you know which person in the family you act most like?
- Do you know some of the things that happened to your mom or dad when they were in school?
- Do you know some of the jobs that your parents had when they were young?

The children who possessed knowledge of the history of the family had more confidence, fewer emotional problems, and even less depression. They were able to create stronger self-identities by relating their sense of self with the history of their families. Interestingly, the stories that work best are those of family members who struggled and came out ahead. These stories empowered children more than stories that followed a plot structure of persistent success.

We can easily see how this intersects with the issues of perfectionism. When children grow up on a diet of stories of relatives who eventually succeeded or persevered despite tremendous challenge, they can see their own struggles as a natural consequence of life, rather than a personal failing. It sounds overly simplistic when you state it plainly, yet the research at Emory shows that kids simply do better when they know about their families. Families can combine the habit of sharing meals with the storytelling habit. By asking children Emory University's same twenty questions, we can learn the gaps our children have in their own family narrative.

Educators can elicit responses to the questions as well, encouraging children to anchor themselves in their families' histories. Of course, they must be sensitive to the family situations of their students so as not to shame or embarrass anyone. Educators can work with students to build a classroom narrative through shared traditions and stories. When students know stories of others' struggles, they realize their own struggles are the norm, not an exception.

At the end of every school year, I give students a form to fill out that asks about their experiences in the class. The form asks them everything from their favorite assignment we did, to the hardest task of the year, to advice they have for incoming students. Their anonymous responses are hole-punched and corralled in a large binder that is on display at all times. Students frequently flip through the binder, laughing and commiserating with the experiences of students who came before them. I invite former students to visit and share with current students. In short, I make a conscious effort to make it mean something to have been in my class. I've even had years where students created Facebook groups so they could continue to connect long after they moved on.

In my classroom, occasionally a student would whine or complain about the rigor (or sometimes the silliness) of an assignment. I would always respond with the saying, "Your whining is inconsistent with the spirit of learning that exists in this classroom." Eventually, the other students would say it to each other. Even years later, when students see me in the grocery store, many will walk by and say, "Your whining…" and smile. Traditions can be as simple as sayings, as easy as inside jokes. For both parents and teachers, the power of narrative can be an important weapon in the battle against perfectionism.

Lickerman's Model

A hallmark trait of resilient individuals is that they have a strong feeling of control over their lives. This is the opposite of perfectionism, when people can feel that no matter what they do, it will never be enough. Two different strategies can be used to increase personal feelings of control. Both strategies, one from physician and author Alex Lickerman, and one from psychologist Robert Sternberg, are appropriate for use at home and at school.

The first strategy—Lickerman's Model—is a self-reflection sequence of questions that youth (or adults) can ask themselves when they are in difficult circumstances. Specifically in the realm of perfectionism, the questions can be asked when someone feels defeated, discouraged, or frustrated. They can be asked orally, or they can be used for written self-reflection in a journal. Although there are three questions, they do not need to be asked in any particular order, nor does every question need to be asked in every situation.

The first question is: How can my current circumstances help me develop myself? If we can identify what we are learning from an experience, we can often grab victory from what appears to be certain defeat. Notice that the question emphasizes the temporary nature of the circumstances. They are "current," not permanent. The connotation is that the situation is temporary and will change. In the meantime, how can I get something out of it that may help me in the future? One of the benefits of Lickerman's questions is that they focus on actions, not simply emotions. That makes the person him or herself the locus of control.

The second question is: How can my current circumstances help me contribute to the happiness of someone else? Even though we simply cannot find self-benefit in a task or activity, we can salvage value by finding a way to use the experience to help others. As we discussed in Chapter 6, many gifted children identify with the needs of others to a greater extent than is typical. For these individuals, this second question can be particularly useful. Even if I failed in my attempt, I have something of value I can bring back to others, even if it is only information on how they can avoid failure in the same activity. For some individuals, even if they can't be successful, they can find power in serving as a cautionary tale.

The last question is: How would the wisest person on earth look at my current circumstance, and what would that wise person do in my stead? This question separates the ideas of "smart" and "wise." The use of the word "wise" implies evaluation and maturity. The first part of the question emphasizes the importance of perspective. One thing that blocks perfectionists is an inability to see things from helpful perspectives, or any perspective other than that of all-or-nothing, take-no-prisoners, zero-sum-game success or failure. Like the other questions, it is action-focused. Notice the second part of the question: what would the wise person *do*?

Sternberg's Model

Psychologist Robert Sternberg's ideas regarding adaptive intelligence can help in situations that arouse perfectionistic tendencies. Adaptive intelligence is part of Sternberg's Triarchic Theory of Intelligence,[57] developed when he was a professor at Yale University. Interestingly, Sternberg himself came to study intelligence through a circumstance that would awaken the latent perfectionist in many people. In elementary school, Sternberg did not do well on IQ tests he was administered, due to severe test anxiety, and he felt keenly the diminished expectations his teachers had of him because of his low scores. Eventually, a teacher realized his potential, changing the course of his life. Because of these early experiences, he became interested in intelligence and how it was measured, inspiring his theory.

Sternberg describes intelligence as having three components. First, Analytical Intelligence is the kind of intelligence that takes a problem and finds its answer. The second, Creative Intelligence is used when you don't know for sure if there is a solution. If you have seen the movie *Apollo 13*, you may remember the scene at Johnson Space Center when the astronauts are on the dark side of the moon in a broken spaceship. A group of engineers gather in a room with a pile of random parts piled on a table. This is what they have, the engineers are told. Figure out how they can fix it. That's Creative Intelligence.

The third part (hence, Triarchic) of Sternberg's model is Adaptive Intelligence—the kind of intelligence that enables people to live in an environment that works for them. If someone's environment is not working for them, three reasonable possibilities exist. The first is, "Can I change myself to better fit the environment?" Sternberg calls this "adaptation." For instance, if a child is feeling bored in a class, he or she may decide to implement strategies to manage the boredom, rather than complain or become disruptive.

The second possibility is to ask, "Can I change my environment?" which Sternberg calls "shaping." Youth may be less able to shape their environments than adults are, but if they can figure out ways to do it appropriately, it can benefit them in developing resilience. When Crystal's older brother went off to college, she came home from school to an empty house. Although old enough to stay alone until her parents got home from work, she found herself feeling lonely. Her perfectionism flared, and she began to feel out of control. She approached her parents with a plan: she wanted a dog. She listed the costs and responsibilities, and divided them up between those she could take care of and those for which she would need her parents' help. After some discussion, they agreed. Crystal found that coming home to a dog felt much less lonely. A side effect of getting the dog was that Crystal realized how much she loved him, despite his chewing her favorite shoes and other less-than perfect puppy behavior, and she was able to transfer this understanding to herself and realize that people could love her in spite of her imperfections.

If you cannot adapt yourself to the environment and you cannot adapt the environment to better fit you, the third option in Sternberg's model is to leave, what he calls "selection." This may mean moving to a different class, a different school, or homeschooling if the school situation isn't working. It can mean abandoning unhealthy relationships as well. Like shaping, selection may not be under the control of children. To build a child's sense of control, allow children the opportunity to have a voice in the selection of their physical and personal environments as early as the maturity of the child allows.

I think of Sternberg's ideas of Adaptive Intelligence as "Kenny Rogers' Intelligence" – you gotta know when to hold 'em, know when to fold 'em, know when to walk away and know when to run. When people lack this type of intelligence, they find themselves feeling anxious in situations they can't control and in relationships that don't really work for them. This can breed perfectionism as they struggle to make untenable situations work by over-adapting.

The Right Kind of Optimism

In his book *Good to Great*, James Collins shares the story of Admiral James Stockdale, the highest ranking military officer held captive in Vietnam. A prisoner of war in the infamous Hanoi Hilton, Stockdale told Collins one of the factors that helped him survive the ordeal. Many of the prisoners had a belief in their imminent rescue; they were naïve, unreasonable optimists. Certainly they would be rescued by the Fourth of July. No? Then surely by Thanksgiving or Christmas. When these anticipated days came and went, they lost hope. In a place like the Hanoi Hilton, a loss of hope could lead to despair and even death. Those who survived were those who had a more practical form of optimism. They had faith in the end of the story. They believed that they would ultimately be rescued, but that it would be a long, hard road until then.

Perfectionists need this kind of practical optimism. Too often, perfectionists believe that everything will be okay only if each individual assignment earns the highest grade possible, where every report card looks like a typewriter stuck on the letter "A." Far healthier is the mental framework of Stockdale's kind of optimism. When they can say, and mean,

"This is going to be long and hard, but in the end, it will work out," they are far less likely to give up, to drown in discouragement, or to see their identity as being reflected in performance of every task.

The Skill Acquisition Timeline

Karim's parents were worried because he had fallen into a pattern they found worrisome. Whenever he turned in an assignment, he would wait anxiously until he got the grade back, always sure it would be a 100. Even a ninety-eight would send him to the teacher's desk in tears. He was on a constant emotional roller coaster; his optimistic hope swelled and then was dashed. He started doing poorly on assignments on purpose to avoid creating hope, only to see it destroyed. Because only perfect scores satisfied him, he spent most of his time being disappointed.

Things came to a head when one of his teachers began offering extra credit on tests built in to the test itself. Now, even a 100 wouldn't satisfy him. After his mother read *Good to Great* for a discussion group at work, she told her husband about what Collins called "The Stockdale Paradox" about the toxic nature of unreasonable optimism. They realized that they could influence Karim, gently leading him to more reasonable optimism. They had some success using Barbara Clark's model discussed in Chapter 7, but they knew they needed something more concrete for their very literal son. They found what they were looking for in the Skill Acquisition Timeline.

Most of us, especially those of us with perfectionistic tendencies, have inaccurate ideas about the *process* of acquisition of skills. We tend to over-focus on the stage of development we're in at the moment, and undervalue the work it took to get to the current stage. Because of that, we often find ourselves frustrated with the challenges posed by what we're learning right now, forgetting that as hard as this seems now, in the future it will seem as easy as what we learned ten years ago.

To break this habit, create a timeline of the learning process of the activity.[58] Begin the timeline by writing down what you are learning now. Then, think about what you learned right before what you're learning now, and continue to move backwards until you get to the earliest thing you can think of that you ever learned related to it. Then, jump forward to what you know or guess might come next in your learning or growth in that activity. On the timeline, block off proportional periods of time for each stage, meaning that if you were in one stage for a long time, make that section of the timeline reflect that. Effective timelines have at least six sections (four previous, one current, one future).

When you do this over and over, a few valuable things become clear. First, you begin to see that it is a waste of energy to stress about how hard something seems right now, because at some point in the future it will feel easy. You learn that there is no such thing as hard or easy; there is simply familiar and unfamiliar. Second, you realize that you will be in different stages for different lengths of time. You may think that you are stuck in a stage and will never move on, but if you look back and see that in previous times you were in a certain stage for a long time as well, it can help you avoid discouragement. Similarly, looking forward to what is coming up can lure you out of frustration. You come to realize, "Yes, I'm tired of doing this right now, but if I hang in there, soon I'll be able to do *xyz*." This can help us overcome the perfection-induced doldrums. There are more benefits to the timeline exercise, yet these three are of most use in addressing perfectionism.

Following are two possible timelines. Imagine we're doing a timeline for reading.

We start where we are in that skill, placing it fairly far to the right side of the timeline (because the only thing that is going to go farther to the right is the future).

				I am reading classic novels.	

Next, add in what came just before this.

			I read longer books with no pictures.	I am reading classic novels.	

Continue adding what came before.

My parents read to me.	I began to learn to read.	I read picture books.	I read chapter books.	I got hooked on the *Redwall* series.	I read longer books with no pictures.	I am reading classic novels.	

Lastly, add what you think the next step in your learning will be.

My parents read to me.	I began to learn to read.	I read picture books.	I read chapter books.	I got hooked on the *Redwall* series.	I read longer books with no pictures.	I am reading classic novels.	I will read *War and Peace*.

Notice the different widths of the columns; this represents different periods of time in different development stages. It is vital that youth understand that not all concepts or skills will be acquired or learned at a particular pace.

Let's look at another example—a timeline of piano skill. Again, we begin with where we are currently.

				I playing songs I know from musicals.	

Next, we add what we learned just before this.

I liked to sing little songs and listen to my mom sing.	I got a toy xylophone.	I started taking piano lessons.	I finished Levels 1 - 6 of my piano books.	I am playing songs I know from musicals.	

Lastly, add the next step. This can be a goal or a logical next step.

I liked to sing little songs and listen to my mom sing.	I got a toy xylophone.	I started taking piano lessons.	I finished Levels 1 - 6 of my piano books.	I am playing songs I know from musicals.	I will play a simplified version of *Jupiter* from Holst's *The Planets.*

You can make the timelines visually pleasing by using color or illustrating them, or even create and display them in PowerPoint with an entire presentation full of multiple timelines. Have children update the timelines periodically so they can see where they have come and anticipate where they are going. This exercise is most effective if parents participate as well, creating their own timelines, even if the specific task is not something the child fully comprehends. My husband is a software developer, so his timelines are Greek to me (English major!), yet it still helps if I see that he, too, has grown his skills and continues to grow them.

Getting Back Up

When I was little, I had a toy that was a blow-up Bozo the Clown with sand in its bottom. You may remember that toy as well. You may also remember Weebles. I loved Weebles. I actually still have a Weeble, and I still like it. I like Weebles because when you knock them, they get right back up. They don't stay down for a second. My Bozo the Clown toy was similar. Once it was blown up, you could punch it, and it would knock down to the ground. Then, like magic, it would come back up again. The beauty of both toys was that they simply could not be permanently knocked down. They would always rise, like little beautiful momentum physics experiments.

We want to be a little bit like Weebles and Bozos. We are actually designed to be like Weebles and Bozos. The thing that made the Weebles and Bozos bounce back up was their fat, round bottoms. What allows people to get back up is resilience. Do you remember the jingle, "Weebles wobble, but they don't fall down"? It was catchy, and it's true. Weebles would have been no fun at all if they didn't knock down. When faced with challenge, we need to channel our inner Weeble. We can make the Weeble song our own song. We wobble, but we don't fall down.

We can buy a Weeble, and we can say to kids (or even ourselves) when something goes wrong, "Oh, it looks like something knocked over your Weeble," as we wobble it back and forth. You've got a bad grade on this, or not the grade you were hoping for. You didn't make the soccer team. You didn't get invited to the birthday party. You weren't able to make your poster look the way you wanted. Let them physically knock over the Weeble. We remind kids that when Weebles get knocked over, they get right back up again. Ask them, "How are you going to do that? How will you rock back up?" We want to teach our kids to rock back up when they get knocked down. Weebles were designed to get knocked down and get up again, and so were people. Weebles that never fall over are just paperweights

Resilience is made of ordinary magic. It is lemonade stands in front yards. It's finding the motivation to overcome discouragement when we don't make a team or a play we try out for. It's finding a new friend when an old, trusted friend deserts us. It's raising our hand again after being embarrassed in class. It's built around family dinner tables and in the telling of stories and the creation of timelines. It's learning to be a little more Weeble-like. When we practice the skills of resilience, we ward off perfectionism, partly because it loses its power over us.

Key Ideas:

- Building resilience is especially important in people struggling with perfectionism.
- Persistent, long-term stress can affect the epigenetics of children, decreasing resilience even into adulthood.
- Family mealtimes are protective and beneficial in building resilience.
- Children are strengthened by knowledge of their family's stories.
- Creating a Skill Acquisition Timeline can improve perspective and help people move through frustrations in the learning process.

Action Steps:

- Decide to develop a stronger family mealtime habit. Resolve to eat together a certain number of meals per week and the follow through.
- Develop a family storytelling tradition. Ask grandparents about stories from when they were young, recording them if possible.
- Ask your children the twenty questions from the Emory study to gauge their knowledge of the family narrative.
- Create Skill Acquisition Timelines for every member of the family.
- Consider acquiring a Weeble (or similar toy) and using it as a discussion prompt for overcoming disappointment.
- Read the American Psychological Association's *Resilience Guide for Parents and Teachers.*[59]

Parenting and Teaching the Perfectionist

CHAPTER IX

Perfectionism is the voice of the oppressor.

- ANNE LAMOTT

Parenting and educating perfectionistic children is not for the faint of heart. If parents, by nature, are not at all perfectionistic, the intensity of the perfectionistic child can be exhausting, overwhelming, and bewildering. Why can't he just relax a little? Why does he practically make himself sick over these weekly school assignments? Why does everything have to be so intense?

Parents who struggle with their own perfectionism may feel guilty, worrying that the child has inherited the perfectionism gene from them or that they have turned their home into a greenhouse that grows perfectionism. Teachers can feel defensive, hesitant to grade or to return less-than-perfect work, waiting for the tantrum that will follow. They may worry the parents will blame them if the child achieves less than a perfect score, a fear nearly every teacher has realized at some point.

There are, however, some "best practices" in the care and feeding of perfectionistic gifted children, though like other strategies in this book, not all of them will work with all children. Choose the ones that work for you, and save the others for another time, or share them with a friend who may find them useful.

Positive Priming

Melissa Masterson, who teaches fifth grade science at a gifted magnet school, has worked with more than her share of perfectionists. At a workshop, she heard about a study[60] done by researcher Sara Bengtsson on something called "positive priming" and decided to try it in her class. In Bengtsson's study, the researchers "primed" college students with words like "smart," "intelligent," and "clever" right before a test. Another group was primed with words like "stupid" and "ignorant." The students weren't told they *were* those things; the words were simply used in the classroom. Bengtsson and her colleagues found that the groups responded differently to mistakes based on how they were primed with the words used in conversation. This difference was even visible in fMRI (functional magnetic resonance imaging) scans of their brains.

While traditional MRI scans look at anatomical structures of the brain (or whatever they're scanning), fMRI scans[61] look at blood flow. Blood traveling from the lungs, freshly loaded with oxygen, responds differently to the super strong magnetization of the MRI machine than does blood that is poorly oxygenated. When we are using a part of our brain, blood flows to that part to bring oxygen and glucose to fuel the neurons, and fMRI scans can detect what parts of a person's brain are being used during the scan. The signal the scan is looking for is called the blood-oxygen-level-dependent signal, or BOLD signal.

Bengtsson's study wanted to see specifically what happened in the brain when a person taking a test realized he had made a mistake. Interestingly, when the mistake followed positive priming, the anterior medial part of the prefrontal cortex (involved in self-reflection) was active.

It seems as if the brain, primed by positivity, was surprised by an error and worked to correct it. "Wait!," the brain seemed to say. "I was supposed to be able to do that. Let me play with it a little more." If the student was primed negatively, there was no flaring there. It was as if the brain had no expectation of doing well and was unsurprised by failure.

Melissa Masterson decided to see if she could apply this study in her classroom to benefit students struggling with perfectionism. First, she described the study to her students, and they discussed its ramifications. That discussion alone yielded great results. On test days, she would put up a sign she made that said, "Stuck? Light up your anterior medial prefrontal cortex!" She even made a sign for the door of the classroom that read, "Our anterior medial prefrontal cortexes are all lit up. Are yours?" She purchased die cuts of light bulbs and would lay them on the desks of students who were taking the time to work through difficult problems. It was, she said, like "neuroscience meets schoolhouse magic."

It worked so well that she asked her students if they wanted to try to reproduce Bengtsson's study, without an fMRI. They would use data instead. The students excitedly worked out a plan where they wrote short scripts for teachers to read prior to test experiences. Using multiple teachers from the same grade, they did A/B testing, having some teachers use positive priming and others use negative priming. They repeated the experiment four times, with teachers using both types of priming twice, but in a different order. Melissa's students gathered compared performance of the students under different priming environments and presented the data to the faculty at a staff meeting. The results? Students who were primed positively had class averages on the assessments that were six points higher, on average, than classes that were primed with negative word messages. In Masterson's own class, the results were even more startling. She didn't even have to keep priming because the awareness that students gained of the connection between how well they thought they would do and how well they actually did was to a great extent under their control.

In addition to using positive priming exactly as Bengtsson and Masterson did, teachers can put positive messages on tests to create the same impact. For example, simply use positive and encouraging words in the directions. Next to tricky problems, add messages using thought bubbles that say things like, "This one takes extra time and may take more than one attempt. You can do it!" Before children leave for school, parents can make sure they use positive words, not just, "Do you have your lunch money?" This is not a *Little Engine that Could* strategy that merely assumes that if you think you can, you can. It is using anticipatory encouragement to harness the power of the brain to help us avoid the defeatism that so often accompanies perfectionism.

Maintain Reasonable Schedules

One day, LaRoyce's teacher asked him to draw a picture of his room. He drew a picture of the inside of his mother's minivan. LaRoyce spends far more time in the van than he does in his actual bedroom. At only five years old, he is overscheduled, as is true for so many modern children.

When our family lived in Germany for a year while I was in the service, the thing I loved best was the slower pace of life. Evenings were spent with a long walk after dinner and family time. Stores were closed on Sundays and late evenings. When I returned to the United States, I remember exclaiming to a friend, "America feels like one big store!" I longed, and still long, for that slower pace and relaxed lifestyle.

We are an overscheduled society, and this applies to both parents and children. Parents need to dial back if their schedules are so busy that the smallest ripple in the pond capsizes the time boat. This isn't just about overscheduled kids; it's about overscheduled families. If you find yourself continually thinking, "It'll calm down after fill-in-the-blank," but yet it never does, you are overscheduled. This may seem like simply an unavoidable facet of modern life, yet I believe it is a critical step in mitigating perfectionism.

Being overscheduled is stressful and generates anxiety, unhealthy habits, or even mental health issues that manifest themselves as attempts to cope with stress or anxiety. When people with anxiety disorders have more stress in their lives, they become *more* anxious. When people with eating disorders have more stress in their lives, their symptoms get worse. When people with perfectionistic tendencies have more stress in their lives, they become even more perfectionistic. As parents, we are the ones who in charge of our children's schedules, and because of this, we wield a lot of influence over their level of stress. Educators similarly influence schedules as well through our assignments of work outside of school. All adults play a role in this particular aspect of the management of perfectionism—too much scheduling and not enough free time.

In 2006, Mental Health America[62] released the results of their survey of 882 children between the ages of nine and thirteen. Of the children surveyed, 41% reported feeling stressed all or most of the time, primarily because they felt overwhelmed with all that they had to do, and 78% of the children longed for more free time. In the years since the poll was conducted, the situation has likely worsened. Children's lives have become even busier and, at the same time, more controlled by the adults in their lives.

Play time and homework also have become more structured. In the 1980s and 1990s, school sports required about ninety minutes per week. After the 1990s, it increased to three hours per week, while children's unstructured play time was cut back by twelve hours per week. Simultaneously, homework time demands increased fifty percent.[63] Today, children under thirteen spend only about a half an hour each week in unstructured outdoor play time. This is distressing because the work of children *is* play. If children do not have unstructured play time, they will suffer. Dr. Kathy Hirsh-Pasek, a psychology professor at Temple University and one of the authors of *Einstein Didn't Use Flashcards*, says, "Play has become a four-letter word in society, yet we suffer from a creativity crisis. We need more play, not less." Few activities are as valuable to a child as play, and its greatest enemy is a lack of time for it.

Another concern is how often children's play is controlled by adults. Gone are the days of children's being told to "go out and play and come home when the street lights come on." When children are overscheduled, with little time for their own, imaginative play, brain development, diminishes. Additionally, when adults control the play, as they do with any organized activity, it sends the message that there is a "right" way to do it. This message implies that they will be evaluated if they don't do it correctly, and it can promote perfectionism.

Perhaps the greatest threat to this kind of play is the constriction of the territory in which children are allowed to roam. In a 1990 British study called "One False Move,"[64] researchers plotted the space across which British children were allowed to go unsupervised. Tracking generations of the same families on maps revealed the incredibly shrinking area in which modern children are allowed to play. In fact, 8-year-olds had 1/9th of the area in which they are allowed to roam as their parents did, and only 10% of them were allowed to go to school unsupervised. Parents worry about their children's safety, yet there are no data to show that children are less safe than they were fifty years ago.

What has changed? Media coverage floods adults (and children) with tales of abductions and accidents, creating worry that something could happen to our child. Social media facilitates vicious criticism on any parent whose child is harmed, instantly heaping blame on the parents, a dynamic that has an oppressive effect on parenting as people worry how their actions will appear to others.

A similar dynamic exists for educators, whose every action is analyzed and often found wanting, usually without full context or information. Some parents who have allowed their children to roam in ways that were completely expected and normal a generation ago have even been charged with neglect. When parents and teachers operate from fearful protectionism, youth suffer, and part of this suffering is an increased expectation your behaviors are being judged and evaluated, and that everyone must do everything exactly right, or else.

One lesson we learned from the Good Samaritan studies[65] is that hurry is the enemy of good intention and impulse. The Good Samaritan studies are named after the Bible story of a Samaritan who encounters on the side of the road a man who has been robbed and beaten up. Although Samaritans were considered unsavory and beneath Jews in status, the Samaritan helped the man, taking him to an inn and paying for his care. In the studies, researchers tested peoples' willingness to stop and render aid to others. Perhaps it will not surprise you that when people were in a hurry, they were far less likely to help others than they were when they had time. Apparently, character is more situationally responsive than we sometimes wish to believe. We like to think that we are nice people, yet the research is clear: when we are rushed, we are rarely our best selves.

When children are rushed, it's even worse. Children's emerging executive functioning skills go into hiding. Fights among siblings break out. Even patient parents find themselves exasperated searching for one lost shoe while the school bus's approach grows closer and closer. There are tears and harsh words that would otherwise not have been said. When children struggle with perfectionism, hurry makes it worse. The added stress, rather than making kids feel like, "Oh well, I'm in a hurry, so I'll just finish it quickly," brings out the perfectionistic tendencies even more, and the child can become almost perverse in her determination to get things just so, even as the parent is in the car in the driveway honking for her to hurry.

Unfortunately, we live in a society that overvalues busy-ness. When we meet people, if even more than a few words are exchanged, the topic soon turns to how busy both parties are. It is a source of pride to be very busy. We rush, rush, rush and overcommit ourselves. We schedule thirty hours of living into twenty-four hours of day. Most dangerously, as the studies reveal, we are imposing this same unhealthy value system to our children. Rare is the family that has more than a single evening free during the week. Practices, lessons, games, and meetings fill already-crowded calendars. Our kids do homework in the school bus or in their parents' cars, papers perched precariously on knees. We practically weep with relief when weather cancels events, until we realize that those cancelled events must be rescheduled and somehow squeezed into bursting calendars. This dynamic is the enemy of all that is mentally and physically healthy for children.

Even though it seems like nothing can be eliminated from busy schedules, it must be done. When parents are overscheduled, their stress makes them unable to easily handle the natural fluidity of a child's needs. Flexibility and schedule rigidity are mutually exclusive. When your schedule has a little wiggle room, you are able to be more flexible. If a child needs an extra few minutes to calm himself when stressed, parents are easily able to provide that time if they planned ahead and padded the schedule.

How do you know if you're overscheduled? You can ask yourself a few telling questions:

- Do you wake up in the night, worried you've forgotten something?
- Do you feel guilty if you sit down and simply do nothing?
- Do you find yourself grabbing fast food on the run because you are too busy to cook or even eat? Are you known by name at the fast food places?

- If you were to get sick, would it cause a scheduling disaster?
- Would it take you a very long time to explain to someone else what your schedule is?
- Do you ever wish you would get a little bit sick so you could have an excuse to stay in bed?
- Do your kids frequently fall asleep in the car?
- Do you often feel like something is chasing you?
- If you were to lose your calendar (or your phone), would you feel tremendous anxiety?

These feelings are incompatible with mental health. Parents must stand against overscheduling children (and themselves), and if the child struggles with perfectionism, it is "mission critical."

Let me introduce you to an underutilized word. It is the word, "no." Saying "no" to too many activities teaches your children the important skill of discernment. When we overcommit ourselves or our children, we are not only negatively affecting them in the moment, but also setting unhealthy patterns for the future. At the root of overscheduling are fear and pride. We are afraid that if our children don't participate in the activities everyone else seems to be participating in, they may not fit in. We worry that if we start baseball "too late," the child will never be able to make the high school team. Too many parents see their children as avatars, overly concerned about what their child's achievements say about them, instead of focusing on the child. Fear and pridefulness are not effective parenting behaviors. We cannot teach children to learn to manage their time if all they see from adults is mismanagement. Overscheduling is a malignant mismanagement of time.

Keep in mind that just because something interests a child, formal instruction or participation is not required, at least not right away. Wait a bit before you sign your child up for something to see if it is a lasting interest. Rent the violin or clarinet; don't buy it. Four-year-olds are just as happy, if not more so, playing informal games of soccer with families or a few friends as they are playing it in formal leagues with practices and regimented games. We do not need to sign kids up for every opportunity that presents itself. If a child shows interest in ballet, basketball, soccer, art, or swimming, engaging in that activity informally as a family works well. Of course, children learn social skills through extra-curricular activities and sports. That benefit will be lost, however, if children (or parents) are so overscheduled that it brings out their worst. Bear in mind that the more organized the activity, the more likely it is to awaken perfectionistic inclinations.

Another danger of overscheduling is the depressive effect it has on the amount of time that children can spend outside. Nature is curative; multiple studies have shown that a person's stress level falls within minutes of being out in natural settings. Even just viewing nature can mitigate stress, and, especially important for our purposes, children who can see and interact with nature show improved ability to pay attention.[66] It is quite likely that we are undermining our children's ability to pay attention by the double blow of asking them to manage too many things while simultaneously robbing them of the opportunity for unstructured outdoor experiences. Parents who resist society's pressures to overschedule their families may find that the benefits far outweigh the difficulty of learning to say no, even to things that seem like good activities. It is not that the activities are bad; it's that unstructured, unhurried lives are better, especially for perfectionists.

Accept that Gifted Children Might Not Like School

Gifted children are no more likely to like school than any other child, perhaps enjoying it less. One meta-analysis[67] looked at the childhoods of more than 700 eminent men and women and found that almost all of them loved learning. However, they often disliked school and their teachers.

Another relevant study[68] compared youth who were intellectually gifted with students who were able and active in arts or athletics. Although they expected to discover passion in both groups of participants (as demonstrated by continually talking about the activity, being very focused on it, feeling joyful about it, and including it in their identity formation), they discovered the opposite among the cognitively gifted. The athletes and dancers were passionate, but "there was little evidence of passion among the gifted youth" with regard to schoolwork and "many of the gifted students had difficulty identifying aspects of school that interested or excited them."

In some ways, though, this was an inappropriate comparison. The gifted children were expected to be passionate about a forced activity (school) simply because they had high ability in one aspect (intelligence) that is necessary for school success, but which does not necessarily fit with their areas of passion.

Miriam Adderholdt addresses many of the reasons perfectionistic kids might not like school and how perfectionism can actually lead to dislike of school. She discusses learning approaches and school habits (even relying too much on caffeine) that can plague perfectionists and how to avoid or mitigate them.[69] The book is geared to teen readers, but if you teach or parent younger children, you can read the book yourself and then translate her information and strategies into appropriate language for younger children.

The same technique (read and translate) can be used with Dan Willingham's *Why Don't Students Like School?*[70] Willingham, a professor of psychology at the University of Virginia, explores the neuroscience of the disconnect between learning and school. This powerful book is a must-read, particularly for teachers. For parents, it can help you understand why a child who is autodidactic at home and readily (even eagerly) seeks learning opportunities outside of school languishes in a classroom environment. For both parents and teachers, Willingham's idea that we don't need to constantly be connecting learning to the students' interests and daily lives is interesting and worth exploring. He argues, "If I'm continually trying to build bridges between students' daily lives and their school subjects, the students may get the message that school is always about them, whereas I think there is value, interest, and beauty in learning about things that don't have much to do with me." Parents and teachers play a role in leading kids to this mindset about school.

Academic ability is a complex interdependence of intellectual and social skill, and cognitive intelligence in isolation rarely yields great results. Part of school success is intelligence, but also important are the ability to operate and cooperate within a group, a willingness to show respect for others' property and feelings, and patience with process. Children whose parents or teachers expect that intellectual giftedness alone should equate with school success often miss the other necessary skills. While it is expected that typical learners will not find school to be their favorite activity, gifted children are often expected to enjoy it. This disconnect between expectation and reality can either increase a students' school-based perfectionism or cause a complete rejection of the system altogether.

School and learning are two very different activities. Parents and teachers who can accept that are better positioned to be able to help the student build other skills necessary to enjoy success. Because our brains are wired to enjoy success, students who possess the skills to succeed and do succeed will enjoy the activity more.

Facilitate Group Work Effectively

Makayla was frequently criticized by her teachers for her inability to work in groups effectively. It was becoming increasingly an issue because once she reached middle school, some of her classes were counting towards her high school grade point average and would influence college admissions. Since many of her classes included small group assignments and cooperative learning activities, her struggles were having a negative impact on her grades. When her parents asked for my help with the situation, their first thought was that Makayla needed to develop more social skills. They were wrong. Her teachers were the ones who needed more skills.

Working well in a group is a necessary social skill—at least enough to have "business-friendly" skills. Social skills are essential for success, particularly since group work is a common instructional model. However, many (perhaps even most) educators do not consciously set up the students for success within the group, and it was this dynamic that was undermining Makayla.

Small group instruction, called "cooperative learning" in the education community, is an instructional strategy where small groups of students work together to complete an assignment or task. The tasks can be small, discrete activities, such as a single problem, or they can be extended projects that last for weeks. There are best practices in cooperative learning that must be followed if social dynamics are to work well, yet these are rarely followed. Perhaps the most important of these practices is that roles within groups must be clearly established, so that each student is responsible for his or her own grade. Instead, Makayla was required to work in groups where her grade depended upon the work of others. Many times, students who knew her skill and task commitment would surrender their work to her, leaving her to shoulder a vastly disparate quantity of the work. She would then be accused by teachers of "taking over." This is unfair. Anyone, even an adult, would naturally "take over" if their pay, which is what a grade is, were tied to another's work, especially if the person knew her skills were superior and likely to result in a better outcome. That's common sense, not arrogance or bossiness.

Another issue was that the teachers were not instructing students on the skills of working within a group. Taking turns and sharing ideas in a respectful way is not necessarily natural behavior. It only takes a cursory glance at Facebook to see that that is true. Teachers and parents must explicitly teach children how to listen politely and demonstrate exactly what that looks like. In our culture, listening is as much of an eye exercise as an ear exercise. We must teach behaviors like eye contact, not interrupting, giving non-verbal signals that we are listening, and not dominating the conversation (I'm still working on this one myself, actually). We can't just throw kids into a group situation with no training in group dynamics, and then criticize them when they don't do well in it.

Gifted children also deserve the right to work with intellectual peers. They should not always be asked to work in groups with mixed ability students. Yes, that's great sometimes. We all need to learn to work with lots of different people, but we also need to work with intellectual peers. They have the right to grow as individuals and to be challenged as well. When gifted students who struggle with perfectionism are consistently put in groups where they are the person with the highest ability, they may not perform in socially acceptable ways, and that is not their fault.

It is important to set students up for success in group work, not contribute (even inadvertently) to their failure. I communicated with Makayla's teachers and Makayla herself over the phone. The teachers began to massage the way they organized the groups, and Makayla tried harder to pay attention to how much she was talking versus the other students in her groups. Over the next few months, Makayla's group work skills improved, and, together with the changes made by the teachers, the situation improved immensely.

Implement Appreciative Inquiry

The idea of strengths-based growth, so prevalent now, arose in 1987 when two researchers at Case Western Reserve University had an idea. They felt that problem solving had a problem: it was too negative. The researchers, David Cooperrider and Suresh Srivastva, developed a model[71] called "Appreciative Inquiry" (AI), in which four processes guide change. These processes are:

- DISCOVER: Find out what is working well
- DREAM: Envision what could work well in the future
- DESIGN: Plan out how things could work well (the process)
- DESTINY (or DEPLOY): Carry out the design

The questions being asked are strongly emphasized because the questions have power to guide thoughts and actions in one direction or another. Because of that, it is important to ask positively framed questions. Rather than look at what is broken, you begin with asking what is working well. This is an essential quality of the first step—Discover.

Here is an example of using the AI model to help a group of gifted students as they moved from middle to high school. They were nervous, and their perfectionism was igniting like a solar flare. The goal was to work together to:

- Discover what had worked well for them in junior high.
- Dream of what high school could be like.
- Design a plan to help each student embrace high school.

- Deploy the ideas as the year began and then check back at Thanksgiving break to revisit.

Remembering the emphasis on the power of the questions, these questions were used to guide the conversations with the students for steps one and two—Discover and Dream:

- Why do you like coming to school now?
- What's your favorite part of middle school?
- What do you like most about your favorite teacher?
- What do you think your teachers like about you?
- What do you think are your three best traits that help you succeed in middle school?
- When you are at your best, what do you love most about learning?
- Tell me a story you've told your family about something good that's happened to you at school?
- I'm your fairy godmother, and I'm granting you three wishes for high school. What would your wishes be?
- What do you think the best part of high school will be?
- What subjects do you think you will like best?
- What things do you envision in your backpack or locker in high school?
- What would be the best possible clubs or activities you would want to join or participate in?
- Who would you most want to hang out with or eat lunch with?

Once this discussion has occurred, we move to the third step, Design. Using the responses gleaned, we made a plan. The plan had only three points to keep it manageable, and each student had his or her own plan, depending upon the responses. Here is the plan developed by Yasin:

- Ask Amir and Kharim if they will join debate with me. If they have other plans, ask Hamza or Nour. If no one else will, I will try it myself and also join one of the clubs they are joining.
- Mow my neighbor's lawn so I can pay the difference between the backpack I really want and the one my parents will pay for.
- Find someone I know who has had all my teachers before and ask their suggestions for how to be successful in those classes.

Will these steps assure Yasin of a glorious high school career? Obviously not. Yet they are powerful, as they are all within his own power or reach, they are all reasonable, and they are all small enough to give him a sense of accomplishment going in. Notice that none of them need to be done "perfectly." Yasin used the fourth step—Deploy—and it was important in helping him shape his Destiny.

The use of the AI framework can be an effective tool for both parents and teachers working with youth because of its simplicity. Simply focusing on positive framing of questioning is so powerful that it can be used even without the final two steps, particularly to improve the discussion when perfectionism threatens to ruin a child's perspective of his or her day. For example, when a child is asked, "So, how was your day?" it is easy to get a response such as, "Terrible." Reframed as, "So, what was the funniest thing you saw in the hall today?" it becomes more difficult to get a fully negative response. Don't get discouraged. Those not used to this model may respond at first with, "Nothing." Don't give up. Keep trying. Keep being positive in the questioning. When there is a challenge ahead, try the entire model. Because gifted kids often like metathinking, or thinking about their own thinking, they may like knowing the name and structure of the model.

Support Executive Functioning Skills

Executive function is the command system of the brain. It "allows people to problem solve in order to achieve a goal, including effectively making myriad micro-decisions involved in successful management of day-to-day life."[72] Just because a child is a perfectionist doesn't mean that the perfectionistic part of their brain has informed the executive functioning skills part. The two are often not even on speaking terms. While adults can be confused by a child who can do complex math but can't remember to brush her teeth, the two tasks are not even remotely similar within the brain. You can be gifted and still have executive functioning issues, even a disorder. Dr. Paul Beljan, a neuropsychologist and past president of the American Board of Pediatric Neuropsychology, tells parents and teachers, "Essentially, what is at the core of this deficit is a failure of the brain to consolidate behavior into routines—procedural memory. And if you can't do that, you will have real problems in life, because if I have to cogitate my way through every morning, every morning is different."[73]

Establishing core tasks into routines is necessary if these tasks are to become deeply ingrained and routine in thinking. Combined with that, however, is a need to have enough frequent change to keep the brain interested, so we look at macro structure with micro change. Teachers must set routines for turning in work, for example, yet the ways in which work is reviewed can change from day to day. Similarly, parents will have set bedtime routines, though the story read to the child each night will change.

One tremendous challenge to executive functioning is the trend toward very early departmentalization of subjects in school. Second graders move from class to class, and thus must manage multiple teachers' styles, rules, and expectations, as well as navigate the organizational structures of their schedules. This is an unreasonable demand on a seven-year-old brain, and allowances must be made. For example, teachers of younger students should align their daily routines and discipline expectations so that students don't have to master multiple procedures and diverse expectations. Flexible strategies should be in place to make it likely that the student will be successful, such as in methods of communicating expected work and needed materials. Horizontal alignment of assignments should ensure that students don't have several projects due in different classes simultaneously. Teachers should communicate a student's struggles early, well before failure. The naive idea that children should be "old enough" to manage their own work simply creates frustration and ends up taking more time for everyone. Anything parents and teachers can do to support the child's ability to self-manage his or her own life appropriately can help build these skills in a safe and supportive atmosphere.

Avoid Over-Advocacy

A few years ago, an amazing teacher I knew left teaching gifted children and returned to the regular or on-level classroom. I was surprised, as she herself is gifted and was truly wonderful with the rapid learning and accelerated kids. When I asked her about the shift, she said, "I'll teach gifted kids again when I can teach in an orphanage"—in other words, kids without parents. Ouch! When I consulted on the T.V. show, *Child Genius,* one parent was highly offended by my comment that some parents weren't helicopters; they were hovercraft. She was so upset that she called me on the phone to complain. I still stand by what I said. Unfortunately, parents sometimes find themselves over-advocating, burning bridges rather than building them with the people with whom they most need connection to meet the needs of their child.

Any real or perceived vulnerability on the part of a child tends to elicit protectiveness by parents, a natural response. With gifted children, it is natural for parents to become frustrated with educational systems that seem least able to address the needs of the most able, and sometimes parents and educators engage in a test of wills despite the fact that they share the same goal of student success. The old adage that "little pitchers have big ears" is doubly true for gifted children, and parents who think that their own negative feelings towards educators have no damaging effect on the child's success in school, both socially and scholastically, may be surprised to find that they themselves have done far more damage than even the most ineffective teacher.

I once heard a story about a person who was walking a tightrope across the Grand Canyon, carrying valuable property that belonged to someone else. The owner of the valuable property did not believe the person walking the tightrope was capable of doing it, and began calling out comments from the side of the canyon, and eventually even shaking the rope on which the person was walking. Eventually a wise onlooker told the rope-shaking owner that his behavior made no sense. The message? The less capable we think a person is, the more they should be encouraged and stabilized when they're carrying something precious of ours—our children. Parents who don't like their children's teachers should avoid rope shaking, as it is counter-productive. That doesn't mean avoiding advocacy or intervening if there is a truly toxic situation. It means showing respect and being reasonable in expectations. Reasonable expectations are not compatible with perfectionism, so kids who grow up in homes where perfection is expected of teachers may come to believe that the same is expected of them.

Avoid Unhealthy Comparisons

Comparison is a natural human trait. We are hard-wired to compare ourselves to others, to compare what we possess to what others have, and even to compare our children to other children. Though common, it's not helpful. In fact, Theodore Roosevelt described comparison as the "thief of joy." When trying to parent or educate those who struggle with perfectionism, we must avoid allowing comparison to steal their joy. This happens when we make seemingly innocuous evaluations, when we only display perfect work, or when we push our children in order to be able to hold our heads high during sideline or carpool lane discussions about what our children are doing. Many of us have caught ourselves saying something like, "When I was your age, I would never…." Comparing our children to ourselves is no less harmful than comparing them to other children their age.

Unhealthy comparison begins as soon as a child is born and rarely stops before we die. It is a root cause of much desperate unhappiness. How do we avoid it? Have a ready response when someone tries to compare achievements or development. The response need not be rude. It can be something like, "Oh, I'm so glad to hear so-and-so is doing well." Simply leave it. Don't engage. I've had people attempt to compare virtually everything about my children, from their height to their grades to their college choices to their sports achievements to the color of their hair. It's impossible to avoid, and it's not all mean-spirited. We often compare to reassure ourselves that we're doing okay, that our children are alright, and that we're on the right track. We need to make a special effort to avoid comparison within hearing of the child. The child has already compared herself to her sibling(s) or others, and hearing another's comparison can only be detrimental.

Even positive comparison can be awkward and uncomfortable for a child, and continually singing your child's praises it is not good for the child. When a child hears us talking about all of their accomplishments, it puts pressure on the child that we may not realize is there. For perfectionists, this can be particularly painful. I am not saying you should avoid celebrating achievements for which your child has worked hard to achieve. I am suggesting you are careful about how and where you share information so that it comes across as celebratory rather than bragging or attempting to demean others, thus avoiding "so what are you going to do next?" pressure on the child.

Recognizing accomplishments can feel awkward, though, because parents of gifted children often feel that if they celebrate their child's achievements, other people do the eye roll, even if it's not obvious. It feels unfair. We must try to understand that it is the comparison game that makes this awkward and uncomfortable. Our only power is to make sure we are sharing from the best of intentions, are supportive of other parents, and are avoiding putting pressure on our children.

Key Ideas:

- Positive Priming has a powerful impact on outcome and can be used by parents and teachers alike.
- Overscheduling increases pressure on parents and children, reduces the opportunity for play, and results in an increase in stress on all parties.
- Children must have time for unstructured play, particularly outside play.
- Not all gifted children will like school. Parents and teachers should work with children to develop skills that make students successful in school and not assume that simply because a child is intelligent that school will be a favorite activity or even a successful one.
- Although group work is an integral part of the contemporary educational system, it must be appropriately structured in order for students to be academically and socially successful.
- To prevent unhealthy dynamics in groups, educators must avoid making students responsible for other students' grades.
- Students must be taught the social skills requited for working in a group.
- The Appreciative Inquiry model (AI) can help children in transitional or stressful situations.
- Gifted children may not have superior executive functioning skills.
- Parents and teachers should support students' executive functioning skills by using appropriate routines.
- Parents should avoid over-advocacy that can damage relationships with teachers.
- Unhealthy comparison exacerbates perfectionism in children, and parents should avoid it as much as possible.

Action Steps:

- Try Positive Priming before an upcoming event or activity or simply in the normal course of the day.
- Evaluate your schedule. As a family, discuss how you can make the schedule less demanding. Make sure there is time for unstructured, preferably outside, play.
- Discuss the dynamics of group work with children, including the skills necessary and hos to practice listening actively. If you are an educator, revise your group work activities to make sure children are responsible for only their own grades and have the skills they need to function in the group. Allow gifted children to work together sometimes.
- Begin using the positive questioning aspect of the Appreciative Inquiry Model. Note how the use of positively framed questions changes the tenor of discussions.
- Before an upcoming transition, try the Appreciative Inquiry Model to come up with a plan for success.
- Evaluate children's executive functioning skills and burdens. What executive functions are they expected to have mastered? What are they responsible for doing with or without parental or teacher support? If there are gaps between expectation and skill, develop routines to support that development.
- Build cooperative teacher-parent relationships. Avoid becoming a rope shaker. Find one way to express support. Avoid any criticism of the teacher in front of the child.
- Decide to be a positive example with regard to comparison. Be supportive of other parents. Avoid comparing children to yourself or to other children. Have a discussion with children about whom they feel compared to and the effect of that comparison. Discuss the role of comparison and when it can be helpful (for instance, if you're racing, you may need to know the time to beat).

Coping Strategies

CHAPTER X

Ring the bells that still can ring
Forget your perfect offering.
There is a crack in everything,
That's how the light gets in.

- LEONARD COHEN "ANTHEM"

The difference between those of us who struggle with perfectionism and those whom we would describe as having healthy high standards primarily boils down to coping strategies. Remember that perfectionism is a continuum, not an either/or dichotomy. There is no practical way to have someone who, by nature, lives on the right side of the perfectionism bell curve move completely to the other side and become a careless, laissez-faire slob who never gets anything done and couldn't care less about grades or their job because a lot of these behaviors are hard-wired in. We're all born with tendencies one way or another, and changing those things completely would require changing the fundamental fact of who we are. Even if we could make such a drastic change in character from one extreme to another, we wouldn't want that. What we want is healthy coping, reasonable standards, and joyful children. Developing good self-management strategies, however, can be a challenge, particularly in gifted children who often are both intense and sensitive. Luckily, there are a wide range of strategies for helping our youth become less perfectionistic.

Maladaptive Strategies

Unfortunately, some attempts at managing perfectionism hurt rather than help. Researchers and mental health professionals call these "maladaptive strategies" where individuals "… may avoid, distract, and escape from anxious events and simultaneously ruminate about the event, thinking to themselves that they will do better next time, or they will plan for the future while still blaming themselves for their inability to meet their towering standards."[74] These maladaptive strategies emphasize avoidance, distraction, escape, and self-blame—as well as distancing. In distancing, the person pretends not to be really involved or emotionally invested at all, so the perceived failure has no meaning, when really it does. Distancing can also be a pretending that one isn't responsible because some other unavoidable factor is at fault.

Because the person's apparent behaviors are presented one way, yet the underlying feelings are completely different, this limits the chances that others will recognize the person's true feelings; thus, they are less likely to intervene or support appropriately. A child who fails at something (or perceives that she does), yet acts as if it doesn't matter, is far less likely to get the support she needs. Even worse, sometimes the person's coping strategy leads to punishment. If a child avoids challenge as a strategy, it can look like laziness or a lack of motivation, which then leads to unhelpful criticism.

In avoidance, the person is less focused on doing well and more focused on avoiding doing it "wrong." If you focus on whether the next thing you do will be wrong, rather than giving it the effort it deserves, the more you are likely to act in restrained ways that diminish performance, to underachieve, have anxiety, show a lack of interest in the activity, or even withdraw completely.

Distraction, escape, and self-blame may also occur, none of which will be helpful to a perfectionistic person. Clearly, it is important for people to learn and implement adaptive, helpful strategies in coping with perfectionistic tendencies.

Model Dealing with Stress

How do you model dealing with stress, whether it's somebody cutting you off in traffic, technology that's not working, or a fire drill in the middle of a really important lesson. Many of us don't overtly share how we deal with stress even with ourselves, much less with our children, yet such sharing can help them handle their own stress. Adults have dozens of micro-modeling opportunities every day. How you model dealing with the everyday, day to day, little five-cent stresses is the way that kids are going to learn how to handle and manage it in their own lives, and it's important that we articulate it. It's important that we say things like, "Wow, did you see how that guy cut me off? It's why we have side mirrors. I'm glad I was paying attention."

If the technology isn't working in class, we can say something like, "Well, I can't get this PowerPoint to work. Let's go on and do something else. I'll go find someone who can look at it during my planning time. Sometimes it just needs another set of eyes."

If we say things like, "You know, for some reason I felt really stressed out today, so when I get home tonight, I'm going to..." And then fill in the blank with whatever it is that you do to decrease stress in your life. Do you take yoga? Do you run? Go to dance class? Read a book? Drink a cup of tea? Take a bath? Watch sports? Surf the net to find cool websites? Do you go watch a TED talk? What do you do to decrease stress? Make sure you're articulating your stress management strategies to the youth in your lives. Our problem-solving strategies are often private events in our own thoughts, and we forget to put them into words so that children can see our thought processes and stress management skills.

Of course, you should only mention stress-reducing activities that are positive and appropriate. If you engage in inappropriate stress-reducing activities, please avoid modeling or talking about those for children. Of course, you should also consider finding new and more appropriate ones for yourself. You cannot say one thing and do another; even young children will notice and be harmed by that duplicity.

Adults also need to teach kids how to avoid self-talk mistakes. One helpful activity is to discuss self-talk, and how often we engage in negative, rather than positive, self-talk. What percentage of your self-talk do you say things in your head like, "I'm going to fail; I'm not as good as others; if I don't do perfectly, it will be a huge catastrophe," and what percent of your self-talk are you saying things like, "I will give it my best effort, which will be good enough; If I don't do perfectly, at least I will be learning a lot; I am fundamentally a really competent and likeable person." Most of us find that self-talk is out of balance. We emphasize self-criticism and drift into a "proportionality error" in our self-talk; some days our self-talk is 80% to 90% negative.

Another self-talk error has been called the "bad-bookkeeping error." In our self-talk, we focus on the one error we made, and neglect to remember all the other times where we did things error-free. It's called "bad bookkeeping" because one mark on the debit side of the ledger seems to wipe out all of our assets, regardless of how many we have, and we focus on the one mistake so much that we let it ruin an entire day, or week, or month.

We also can model out loud our own self-talk, carefully avoiding self-talk errors, or correcting them (out loud) when we do make those errors. Children should not hear, for example, "I'm so stupid," unless it's what we want them to say to themselves. Instead, we might say, (Wow! Did you hear what I said? I know I'm really not stupid; I simply made a mistake. I'll learn from it and make some changes."

One helpful way to get children to think about their self-talk is to ask questions instead of telling them how they *should* feel. It doesn't make you feel any better to have someone tell you, "You shouldn't feel that way." Avoid telling children things like, "You should be happy with a ninety eight" or "You don't need to get a hundred all the time" or "Don't be a perfectionist." These kinds of statements are quite a distance south of helpful. What's more beneficial is a dialogue like this, "I see that you're unhappy with this ninety-eight. What would a 100 have told you that this ninety-eight isn't telling you?" Asking questions, rather than telling, is more effective because no one likes to be told how to feel.

Encourage Social Support

Youth with unhealthy perfectionistic tendencies do not believe they have reliable social support, and they often feel that others are unwilling or unable to help.[75] An implication, then, is that parents and educators may need to be more forthcoming than seems necessary to point out to children that they *do* have social support. Reminding them of individuals, groups, and organizations to which they belong can have a powerful protective effect. Sometimes, too, they may need to be guided to the idea of reliable alliances.

When Victoria was twelve, a good friend betrayed her; the loss of trust and end of the friendship with one of the few friends she had was devastating. Her perfectionism began to spiral out of control, and her parents were desperate for help. One night, as Victoria and her father watched re-runs of a *Survivor* television show, her father pointed out alliances the players formed. Victoria became indignant when one person who had formed an alliance abandoned his partner behind the partner's back. Her father made the connection between the people on the show and what had happened to Victoria, and they talked about the differences between a reliable alliance and an unreliable alliance. The conversation led to discussing people in Victoria's life with whom she had reliable alliances, such as her family and two friends. A few episodes further in their *Survivor* marathon, Victoria turned to her dad and said, "I think that when you form alliances, you have to realize that they may not hold, but that doesn't mean you are bad." From that day on, the family used "reliable alliance" as a discussion point, and Victoria slowly healed from the betrayal.

Adults can and should assist youth in seeking social support. Frequently, we see statements, videos, or visuals admonishing people to seek out and be friendly to loners. The example of the child eating alone in the cafeteria is often used. Of course, we should teach children to be friendly and reach out, yet the child sitting alone has a responsibility, too, as do the adults in that child's life. To nurture social support, we must help children discover how to seek it. Part of this is identifying who is on the child's "team," and part of it is helping the child learn the skills of the emotional ecology of the environment. I remember my then seven-year-old son Jonathan telling me, "Mom, the cafeteria is my most difficult society." When we know the "difficult society" of our children, we can use the Appreciative Inquiry method to create a plan to cope with it in an effective way.

When sixteen-year-old Natalie Hampton found herself ostracized and bullied, she created an app called "Sit With Us" that connects kids to other kids with whom they can eat in school cafeterias.[76] Natalie had learned that just going up and asking if she could sit with someone often led to rejection. Adults can help children navigate that dynamic, practicing what to say, how to handle it, and how to arrange someone with whom to sit prior to the actual lunchtime. Why do I suggest that a child who may be being bullied or suffering needs to work towards a solution along with others? Because in life, there will always be other cafeterias. These are not isolated situations. Rarely is the child alone in the cafeteria through personal preference. More often, other social struggles are present as well, and their chronological-age peers are not likely to resolve the issue for them. Even if their peers did help, the resolution depended on others, and was therefore a temporary solution. Other issues are likely involved here. Some kids actually prefer sitting alone, finding the forced togetherness of an entire day at school too much stimulation. Others have mental health issues that make it difficult for them to accept overtures of friendship. The central idea here is that discovering social support is a key coping strategy.

Organizational psychologists know that one key to motivating employees is corporate identity. At home and school, this fundamental social support is called a team. In the movie *Miracle*, the coach knows he can't mold a great Olympic hockey team until they stop seeing themselves as individual players who represent their respective colleges. Instead, they must form a new identity. After a game, he asks them, "Who do you play for?" They answer the names of their universities. Frustrated, he works them and works them until they are exhausted from effort and his assistant coaches are in a frenzy. Finally, the horror is over when one of the players says his name, followed by, "I play for the United States of America" rather than his college. When trying to create an environment in which social support is recognized, help kids answer the question, "Who do you play for?" Help them find their team.

Cultivate and Value Work

We need to feel good about the work we're doing, whether we are four years old or 40 or 60. What makes us feel good about *our* work? Constant progress and a feeling of purpose release the dopamine we need that then encourages us to work more. Dan Ariely, a social psychologist, studied[77] how long people would work on something meaningful versus a task in which they found no meaning. He pulled people into the lab and said, "Build some Lego˚." He told some people that their projects would be unassembled and reused. Others were told that they would just be discarded. They expected that people whose Lego were being discarded would not work very long unless they really loved Lego. But guess what? It didn't matter how much they loved building Lego in general. If they felt the projects were just being discarded, liking Lego was not at all related to whether they would keep working. Since there was no meaning, no purpose, to the work, they didn't want to keep working.

In another experiment, particularly pertinent to teachers, Ariely paid people to complete sheets that required them to identify adjacent duplicate letters. Detailed but boring, and when they turned the papers in, they were offered another paper to complete for a slightly less amount of money. The difference came in how the researchers responded when they received the turned in work. There were three responses: (1) the researchers wrote the name down, scanned the sheet and set it aside; (2) the researchers didn't even look at it, and (3) the researchers not only didn't look at it, they shredded it. As you can probably guess, the people whose work was identified and looked at were willing to do it for much lower pay than the people whose work was ignored or shredded. The message: don't shred the work—literally or figuratively. In the study, ignoring was almost as bad as shredding. Even if people are doing work they otherwise love, say reading, they will not work at it if they find the product of their labors ignored.

Teachers who take long periods of time to return reviewed assignments, expecting students to give full effort to new work in the meantime, will find themselves disappointed. It is difficult to find time to keep up with grading and feedback. However, it makes no sense for teachers to insist that work be turned in on a certain day, often penalizing late work or not accepting it at all, and then not grading it for a week or more. Both parents and teachers should demonstrate value for the work youth do, whether in the school or home. Prove you noticed their efforts, and it will encourage motivation and also help them not feel pressured to do it better and better in the hopes you will eventually notice.

Mental Contrasting

A vital skill tenacious kids possess is mental contrasting—looking at the positive end result while simultaneously keeping in mind the current challenges. That is, they contrast the positive outcome with obstacles that may be in the way. The important work by Angela Duckworth, the Grit researcher, and her colleagues,[78]showed that mental contrasting created "a strong association between future and reality that signals the need to overcome the obstacles in order to attain the desired future." It is the ability to say, "I'm going to finish calculus, even though I know it will take me at least 90 minutes of homework each class."

To practice mental contrasting, you need two things: (1) the goal, and (2) an accurate idea of the challenges or obstacles in the intervening space. This can be as informal as a discussion or as formal as a list posted where the child can see it. Often, this comfort with ambiguity, i.e., that something could be both desirable in the long run and uncomfortable in the short term, can be difficult to understand. It takes practice, and an important part of that practice is reflection. The first time this strategy is used, it helps to do it backwards. Look at something that has recently been accomplished and identify the challenges or obstacles that were in the way. Then, use the same strategy with something upcoming.

Positive Reinterpretation and Reassurance of Worth

The effective strategy of positive reinterpretation, sometimes referred to as "re-framing an experience," allows perfectionists to look at a perceived failure and reimagine it into something that is closer to a growth experience than a failure. The loveliest sympathy card I ever saw read, in part, "I am so sorry for your loss. How amazing it is to have had something so great to lose." This is positive reinterpretation. Changing disappointment in a low grade into a recognition that there will be an opportunity for greater feedback is an example of positive reinterpretation.

Positive reinterpretation occurs after the event, as we look through a different lens at something that has already happened. Positive reframing is essentially the same technique, but is more often applied to something occurring in the present. A basic example of positive reframing is "the glass is half-full, not half-empty," though usually it is more complex than that. Positive reframing is not intended to solve the problem, nor will it, but it will change the focus and the attitude. Hopefully, it will also reduce the damage caused by the incident and build a different, healthier, perspective of the event. Perfectionists more often use negative reframing. Negative reframing is not a technique; it's a predisposition that perfectionists often have. Adults need to help youth gently adjust their reframing practice.

When used appropriately, humor is a great tool for positive reinterpretation and positive reframing. I once saw a professional speaker fall when walking up the steps to the stage in front of hundreds of people, she stood, curtsied prettily, and said, "I will now be taking questions from the floor." Of course, the audience laughed and at the same time forgave her for her misstep. I myself have used the line since. It was so powerful. If we can laugh at ourselves a little, we are better able to positively reinterpret past events and reframe current ones. Like so many techniques in this book, this is best accomplished by children when modeled by adults. Adults who take themselves too seriously send the message to children that every event is potentially catastrophic. They don't even have to have anything actually go wrong, yet still live in fear of its happening. It is like Mark Twain said, "I've lived through some terrible things in my life, some of which actually happened."

To avoid feelings of despair, catastrophic personal failure, and unworthiness, we must keep the focus off of the self and instead focus on the problem. Positive reinterpretation and reframing may require a reminder of the inherent self-worth of the person. None of us is the equivalent of our successes or failures; we have value apart from them, and our worth is separate from what we achieve or fail to achieve. It is important to say things like, "Your effort on this may not have been your best effort, yet you made a choice to spend more time on the other assignment and that paid off. That's part of life, and you handled it well." Sometimes, too, a simple, "I love you and I believe in you" can be strong self-worth medicine.

Making Sure We Are Choosing It

In 1961, the average full-time college student spent twenty-four hours per week studying, not counting class. By 1981, it was down to twenty hours, and in 2003 it was fourteen hours a week.[79] And they weren't working at jobs the other hours; they were socializing. They were gaming. This, as you may have guessed, is not grit.

This is not the line we hear so often about gifted kids not knowing how to study. Let's unpack that argument for a minute because perfectionism takes the blame for gifted students' struggle in college. We talk a lot about how bright kids crash and burn when they get to college because they didn't learn to study when they were in high school, but that's not the full story. In fact, that entire argument seems suspect. If a student is so amazingly intelligent to be able to succeed in classes like Calculus and AP Biology without studying, that person is definitely smart enough to Google, "how to study" and learn how to do it. Frankly, learning to take notes, gather a study group, and read for understanding are skills that are not that complicated. I have taught high school for a very long time, and I have worked with some amazingly intelligent students. I have yet, however, to meet the student who could perform well without studying at all (without cheating). The truth is that many young people aren't prepared to engage in the hard work of university study that requires persistence and grit. They want success, but they don't choose it.

There's a marked difference between wanting something and choosing it. Choosing it involves effort and often sacrifice. Wanting can be done at a safe distance. Sometimes perfectionists want things, but fail to choose them. Then, they are disappointed when they don't get that thing and think it means they have failed. This needs to be reframed realistically as something that was not fully invested in, rather than something that failed. Planning ahead as to how much work a desired achievement will really take and then making a conscious choice to do that work is far more effective coping.

What We Can Learn from Economists

Our oldest son, Gregory, was a Strategy major in college. Sounds cool, doesn't it? It's a business management degree that led him to a wonderful job he loves as an analyst. Along the way, he taught us a few things he learned in economics that easily transfer across disciplines; economic theories and principles can be woven into coping strategies for perfectionism.

The first of these principles is that of sunk cost. Recall all the money spent on musical instruments and those orchestra trips in chapter 4? Sunk costs are costs that have been incurred and cannot be recovered or refunded. Our lives are filled with sunk costs. You know that sweater you have in your closet that you won't get rid of even though you never wear it because you spent so much on it? That's a sunk cost. The same thing goes for the vacuum you've never liked, the expensive kitchen appliance you've never used, and sometimes even a friend who is more frenemy than friend, but you hesitate to end the relationship because you've invested so much in it. Of course, there is a balance. Vince Lombardi said, "The harder you work, the harder it is to surrender," and we've already discussed that tenacity can be a wonderful trait. Where sunk cost comes in is when that tenacity is no longer benefitting you.

Understanding sunk costs is significant because it prevents you from making backward-facing decisions. Making decisions based on time or money that has already been spent hurts us because those decisions are often not in our best interests. Perfectionists have a strong tendency to embrace backward decisions because they are not likely to quit early in the game if they think they can't do it perfectly frequently. Operating our lives based on sunk costs has a tremendous opportunity cost because we lose out on new opportunities because we are clinging to previous choices. Teaching kids about the idea of sunk cost and helping them see when they are making backward decisions can help them avoid these negative consequences.

A second, and related, principle is the idea of diminishing returns, where there is a point at which the benefit gained is less than the amount of money, energy, or time invested. Mastering the law of diminishing returns can benefit perfectionists tremendously. Perfectionists often continue to work on tasks long after that point, essentially wasting time and energy, especially mental energy, in exchange for little or no return. Sometimes, trying to make things better actually makes them worse.

Writing out an actual graph identifying the point at which the time invested no longer makes sense is a helpful tool.

The third economics principle beneficial to perfectionists is one defined by an economist named Vilfreto Pareto. Pareto's principle states that 80% of the benefits will derive from 20% of the investments.[80] The trick is to uncover which 20% are the ones that pay off. All too often, perfectionists engage in all activities with the same energy; they fail to pause and consider which activities are the ones that really pay off and which are simply taking time and energy.

The 80/20 principle isn't simply a rule that applies to school work or money. It also applies to relationships. Most of our social satisfaction is generated by a small number of individuals or interactions or activities. Identifying what those are can clear space in the crowded calendar and can reduce the expenditure of emotional energy, while still feeling emotionally healthy.

Asking yourself a few questions can help you understand what is working. First, "What is the desired outcome?" Next, what is it we are trying to accomplish? An old country saying is, "If you don't where you want to go, any road will do." Then, we need to learn from other people who have accomplished, or are accomplishing, what we want to do. How did they make it happen? Did they go to school for it? Do an apprenticeship? Watch videos on YouTube? Read books or articles? How exactly did they do it? Lastly, "Are the things I'm doing now really helping me, or am I spending the most time and effort on things that matter least?"

Gifted children often love the trivia, the back story, and the inside scoop. At very young ages they can comprehend and apply sophisticated ideas, including principles of economics. This allows us to use those things as a lure, rather than a push, towards success in ways that don't invite perfectionism. Sharing strategies based on economics makes it clear that success does not come from innate ability alone, but rather from deliberate, well-planned effort. Additionally, some people will be more comfortable with the strategies based on the harder science of economics than with touchy-feely ideas, so they relate better to the strategies based on those ideas than the more discussion-based or emotion-based strategies for managing perfectionism. We can share these ideas and practice applying them as part of our toolbox of coping strategies.

The Ultimate Goal

All of the strategies in this book are designed to help people develop a different frame of mind, and they all have a common goal of helping people be able to agree with all of these core statements:

- I evaluate my achievements based on my own standards, not those of others.

- My self-esteem is grounded in many areas of my life, not just my intelligence.

- I am satisfied with a high level of effort, even when it doesn't produce the result I was seeking.

- I avoid excessive self-criticism, and I change my thinking when self-critical thoughts come into my mind.

- I set effective goals for myself, and I don't avoid challenges.

- I can disengage from goals that aren't working well and re-engage with new goals.

- I participate in activities that have no extrinsic reward, like a grade or money.

- I seek help from others when I need it.

- I recognize that if I don't perform well, that does not mean I am bad or lazy.

If all roads really do lead to Rome, these statements are the Rome of managing perfectionism. It is my deepest wish that using the strategies in this book will lead you or the children whom you care for to this kind of feeling. We are not going to find a cure for perfectionism, but we can make—and teach—healthy, beneficial choices and decisions by implementing strategies that work in the particular situation. I hope this book will give you a toolbox full of possibilities.

As the French philosopher Voltaire said, "The perfect is the enemy of the good." I couldn't agree more. A search for perfectionism will almost always lead us to abandon a search for what is good in our lives. It will lead us away from times spent doing good things and having good experiences. If we search for the perfect, we often end up not only overlooking the good, but actually experiencing the bad, the sad, the disappointed, the fearful, and the anxious.

By striving toward goodness and toward excellence, we can develop a willingness to leave perfect alone.

Key Ideas

- Strategies for dealing with perfectionism can be either adaptive or maladaptive. Maladaptive strategies will harm rather than help.
- Adults must model strategies for dealing with stress appropriately and help youth avoid self-talk mistakes.
- People who manage perfectionism well often have strong social support systems, and adults should facilitate growth in this area, helping children develop social skills and identify their team.
- Adults must value the work of children in order to prevent discouragement, a lack of interest, or disengagement.
- The ability to see the end goal as well as the challenges simultaneously is an adaptive coping strategy called "mental contrasting."
- When we positively reinterpret events from the past or positively reframe current events, we can diminish the damage of perfectionistic tendencies.
- It is essential that perfectionists are confident in their inherent self-worth and do not rely on their achievements alone to give them a sense of personal value.
- Sometimes we feel like a failure because we find ourselves doing a great amount of work that is unsatisfying because the work is something we are engaged in without really choosing it.
- The economic principles of sunk cost, diminishing returns, and the Pareto principle are relevant for perfectionists. Adults can share these principles as tools for managing perfectionism.
- The ultimate goal is not to rid oneself of high standards, but rather to seek in mentally healthy ways for the best that is in us.

Action Steps

- Do a maladaptive strategies audit to determine if maladaptive coping strategies are being used. Use the Appreciative Inquiry method or one of the other methods in the book to come up with a plan to mitigate them.
- List appropriate strategies for dealing with stress. Model them. Be open about stress management techniques.
- Identify areas of opportunity in the realm of social support. Does the child need more friends (or even *a* friend)? Does the child need help identifying who is on his/her team? Does the child have certain social situations creating difficulty? Plan for addressing those one at a time, starting with the one causing the most distress.
- Think of three ways you can show that you value the work of children, apart from grades. Possibilities include: discussing what was learned, placing work on the fridge, taking a picture and texting or emailing work to grandparents, or scanning it to keep.
- Practice mental contrasting. Think of a completed goal and the obstacles faced. Then think of a current goal and the obstacles faced.
- Practice positively reinterpreting four past events and reframing one current event.
- Make sure children understand the difference between wanting something and choosing it. List behaviors associated with both choices.
- Share the economics principles of sunk cost, the law of diminishing returns, and the Pareto principle with children.
- Use the three-question model to analyze current projects.
- Consider the core statements and discuss agreement or disagreement with them using a Likert scale (strongly agree/agree/neutral/disagree/strongly disagree).

REFERENCES

American Psychiatric Association. (2013). *Diagnostic and statistical manual of mental disorders DSM-5*. Arlington, VA: American Psychiatric Association.

Adderholt, M., Johnson, D., & Levy, N. (2015). *Perfectionism vs. The Pursuit of Excellence*. Monroe Township, NJ: NL Books LLC.

Adelson, J. L., & Wilson, H. E. (2009). *Letting go of perfect: Overcoming perfectionism in kids*. Waco, TX: Prufrock Press.

Affrunti, N. W., & Woodruff-Borden, J. (2014). Perfectionism in Pediatric Anxiety and Depressive Disorders. *Clinical Child and Family Psychology Review, 17*(3), 299-317. doi:10.1007/s10567-014-0164-4

American Psychological Association Resilience Guide for Parents & Teachers. (n.d.). http://www.apa.org/helpcenter/resilience.aspx

Antony, M., & Swinson, R. (2009). *When Perfect Isn't Good Enough: Strategies for Coping with Perfectionism*. Oakland, CA: New Harbinger Publications.

Ariely, D., Kamenica, E., & Prelec, D. (2008). Man's search for meaning: The case of Legos. *Journal of Economic Behavior & Organization, 67*(3-4), 671-677. doi:10.1016/j.jebo.2008.01.004

Babcock, P., & Marks, M. (2010). The Falling Time Cost of College: Evidence from Half a Century of Time Use Data. doi:10.3386/w15954

Bagot, R. C., van Hasselt, F. N., Champagne, D. L., Meaney, M. J., Krugers, H. J., & Joëls, M. (2009). Maternal care determines rapid effects of stress mediators on synaptic plasticity in adult rat hippocampal dentate gyrus. *Neurobiology of Learning and Memory, 92*(3), 292-300. doi:10.1016/j.nlm.2009.03.004

Bengtsson, S. L., Dolan, R. J., & Passingham, R. E. (2011). Priming for self-esteem influences the monitoring of one's own performance. *Social Cognitive and Affective Neuroscience, 6*(4), 417–425. http://doi.org/10.1093/scan/nsq048

Bluestein, J. (2015). *The perfection deception: why trying to be perfect is sabotaging your relationships, making you sick, and holding your happiness hostage.* Deerfield Beach, FL: Health Communications, Inc.

Bohanek, J. G., Marin, K. A., Fivush, R., & Duke, M. P. (2006). Family Narrative Interaction and Children's Sense of Self. *Family Process, 45*(1), 39-54. doi:10.1111/j.1545-5300.2006.00079.x

Bronson, P., & Merryman, A. (2013). *Top dog: The science of winning and losing.* New York: Twelve.

Brown, D. (2013). *The boys in the boat: Nine Americans and their epic quest for gold at the 1936 Berlin Olympics.* New York: Viking.

Canfield, J., & Wells, H. C. (1976). *100 ways to enhance self-concept in the classroom: A handbook for teachers and parents.* Englewood Cliffs, NJ: Prentice-Hall.

CASA. (2010). *The importance of family dinners VI.* The National Center on Addiction and Substance Abuse, Columbia University. Retrieved from http://www.casacolumbia.org/templates/publications_reports.aspx

Champagne, F. A. (2008) Epigenetic mechanisms and the transgenerational effects of maternal care. *Frontiers in Neuroendocrinology* 29(3): 386-397.

Chambliss, D. F. (1989). The Mundanity of Excellence: An Ethnographic Report on Stratification and Olympic Swimmers. *Sociological Theory, 7*(1), 70. doi:10.2307/202063

Csikszentmihalyi, M. (2009). *Flow: the psychology of optimal experience.* New York: Harper Perennial Modern Classics.

Collins, J. C. (2001). *Good to great: Why some companies make the leap ... and others don't.* New York: HarperBusiness.

Cooperrider, D. L. & Srivastva, S. (1987). Appreciative inquiry in organizational life. In Woodman, R. W. & Pasmore, W.A., *Research in Organizational Change and Development. Vol. 1.* Stamford, CT: JAI Press. pp. 129–169.

Danchin E., Charmantier A., Champagne F. A., Mesoudi, A., Pujol, B., Blanchet, S. (2011) Beyond DNA: Integrating inclusive inheritance into an extended theory of evolution. *Nature Reviews Genetics* 12(7). 475-86.

Daniels, S., and Piechowski, M. M. (2008*). Living with intensity: Understanding the sensitivity, excitability, and emotional development of gifted children, adolescents, and adults.* Scottsdale, AZ: Great Potential Press.

Darley, J. M., & Batson, C. D. (1973). "From Jerusalem to Jericho": A study of situational and dispositional variables in helping behavior. *Journal of Personality and Social Psychology, 27*(1), 100-108. doi:10.1037/h0034449

Duckworth, A. L., Kirby, T. A., Gollwitzer, A., & Oettingen, G. (2013). From Fantasy to Action: Mental Contrasting with Implementation Intentions (MCII) Improves Academic Performance in Children. *Social Psychological and Personality Science, 4*(6), 745-753. doi:10.1177/1948550613476307

Duckworth, A. L., Peterson, C., Matthews, M. D., & Kelly, D. R. (2007). Grit: Perseverance and passion for long-term goals. *Journal of Personality and Social Psychology, 92*(6), 1087-1101. doi:10.1037/0022-3514.92.6.1087

Duckworth, A. (2016). *Grit: The power of passion and perseverance.* New York, NY: Scribner.

Dunkley, D. M., Zuroff, D. C., & Blankstein, K. R. (2003). Self-critical perfectionism and daily affect: Dispositional and situational influences on stress and coping. *Journal of Personality & Social Psychology, 84*(1), 234-252. doi:10.1037//0022-3514.84.1.234

Dweck, C. S. (2006). *Mindset: The new psychology of success.* New York: Random House.

Ericsson, K. A., Krampe, R. T., & Tesch-Römer, C. (1993). The role of deliberate practice in the acquisition of expert performance. Psychological Review, 100(3), 363-406. doi:10.1037//0033-295x.100.3.363

Fitts, P.M., & Posner, M.I. (1967). *Human performance.* Belmont, CA: Brooks Cole.

Foer, J. (2011). *Moonwalking with Einstein: The art and science of remembering everything.* New York: Penguin Press.

Foster, J. F. (2015). *Not now, maybe later: Helping children overcome procrastination.* Tucson, AZ: Great Potential Press.

Fredricks, J. A., Flanagan, K. E., & Alfeld, C. J. (2010). Getting excited about learning: Promoting passion among gifted youth. *Teaching for High Potential*, Winter 2010, 1-12.

Frost, R. O., Heimberg, R. G., Holt, C. S., Mattia, J. I., & Neubauer, A. L. (1993). A comparison of two measures of perfectionism. Personality and Individual Differences, 14, 119–126.

Galbraith, J., & Delisle, J. R. (2015). When gifted kids don't have all the answers: how to meet their social and emotional needs. Minneapolis: Free Spirit Publishing.

Gibbs, N. (2006, June 4). The magic of the family meal. Time. Retrieved from http://content.time.com/time/magazine/article/0,9171,1200760,00.html.

Ginsburg, K. R., Jablow, M. M., & Ginsburg, K. R. (2011). Building resilience in children and teens: Giving kids roots and wings. Elk Grove Village, IL: American Academy of Pediatrics.

Gladwell, M. (2008). Outliers: The story of success. New York: Little, Brown and Co.

Gnilka, P. B., Ashby, J. S., & Noble, C. M. (2012). Multidimensional Perfectionism and Anxiety: Differences Among Individuals with

Perfectionism and Tests of a Coping-Mediation Model. Journal of Counseling & Development, 90(4), 427-436. doi:10.1002/j.1556-6676.2012.00054.x

Goertzel, V., Goertzel, M. G., Goertzel, T. G., & Hansen, A. M. W. (2004). Cradles of eminence: Childhoods of more than 700 famous men and women. Scottsdale, AZ: Great Potential Press.

Gong, X., Fletcher, K. L., & Bolin, J. H. (2015). Dimensions of Perfectionism Mediate the Relationship Between Parenting Styles and Coping. Journal of Counseling & Development, 93(3), 259-268. doi:10.1002/jcad.12024

Greenspon, T. (2007). Adelson, J. L., & Wilson, H. E. (2009). Letting go of perfect: Overcoming perfectionism in kids. Minneapolis: Free Spirit.

Greenspon, T. S., & Samples, P. (2002). Freeing our families from perfectionism. Minneapolis: Free Spirit.

Halsted, J. W. (2002). Some of my best friends are books: Guiding gifted readers from preschool to high school.3rd ed. Scottsdale, AZ: Great Potential Press.

Hampton, N. (2016). Teen Creates "Sit with Us" App for Bullied Kids. Retrieved from http://www.npr.org/2016/09/09/493319114/teen-creates-sit-with-us-app-for-bullied-kids

Hewitt, P. L., Flett, G. L., Turnbull-Donovan, W., & Mikail, S. F. (1991). The Multidimensional Perfectionism Scale: Reliability, validity, and psychometric properties in psychiatric samples. *Psychological Assessment, 3*(3), 464-468. doi:10.1037//1040-3590.3.3.464

Hillman, M., Adams, J., & Whitelegg, J. (2000). One False Move…: Study of Children's Independent Mobility. Policy Studies Institute. Retrieved from http://www.psi.org.uk/pdf/2009/OneFalseMove_Hillman.pdf

Hirsh-Pasek, K., Golinkoff, R. M., & Eyer, D. E. (2004). *Einstein never used flash cards: How our children really learn--and why they need to play more and memorize less.* Emmaus, Pa.: Rodale.

Hofferth, S. & Sandberg, J. (1999). *Changes in American Children's Time, 1981-1997*, Ann Arbor, MI: University of Michigan Institute for Social Research.

Kavaphēs, K. P., & Dalven, R. (1961). *The complete poems of Cavafy*. New York: Harcourt, Brace, & World.

Knowles, J. (1987). *A separate peace*. London: Heinemann.

Lickerman, A. (2012). *The undefeated mind: On the science of constructing an indestructible self*. Deerfield Beach, FL: Health Communications.

Maupin, K. (2014). *Cheating dishonesty, and manipulation: Why bright kids do it*. Tucson, AZ: Great Potential Press.

Mental Health America. (2006). *Mental Health America attitudinal survey: Findings on stress in America*. Alexandria, VA.

National Scientific Council on the Developing Child (2010). *Early Experiences Can Alter Gene Expression and Affect Long-Term Development: Working Paper No. 10.* Retrieved from http://developingchild.harvard.edu/resources/early-experiences-can-alter-gene-expression-and-affect-long-term-development/

Moate, R. M., Gnilka, P. B., West, E. M., & Bruns, K. L. (2016). Stress and Burnout Among Counselor Educators: Differences Between Adaptive Perfectionists, Maladaptive Perfectionists, and Nonperfectionists. *Journal of Counseling & Development, 94*(2), 161-171. doi:10.1002/jcad.12073

Monk, C., Spicer, J., & Champagne, F.A. (2012) Linking prenatal maternal adversity to developmental outcomes in infants: The role of epigenetic pathways. *Development & Psychopathology* 24(4), 1361-1376.

Moore, R. (1999). *Creating a family storytelling tradition: Awakening the hidden storyteller*. Little Rock: August House.

Moore, R. (2005). *Creating a family storytelling tradition*. Atlanta: August House.

Moore, R. (2012, June 26). Email communication.

Neihart, M.. Talent Talk. (2006, August 21). Retrieved March 13, 2016, from https://blogs.tip.duke.edu/giftedtoday/2006/08/21/finding-true-peers-2/

Partnoy, F. (2012). *Wait: The art and science of delay*. New York: PublicAffairs.

Peters, D. B. (2013). *Make your worrier a warrior: a guide to conquering your child's fears*. Tucson, AZ: Great Potential Press.

Preuss, L. J., & Dubow, E. F. (2003). A comparison between intellectually gifted and typical children in their coping responses to a school and peer stressor. *Roeper Review, 26*(2), 105-111.

Resilience Guide for Parents. (2011). American Psychological Association. Retrieved from www.apa.org/helpcenter/resilience.aspx.

Rice, K. G., Kubal, A. E., & Preusser, K. J. (2004). Perfectionism and children's self-concept: Further validation of the Adaptive/ Maladaptive Perfectionism Scale. *Psychology in the Schools, 41*, 279–290.

Sanders, R. (1987). The Pareto Principle: Its Use and Abuse. *Journal of Services Marketing, 1*(2), 37-40. doi:10.1108/eb024706

Schweitzer, A. "Visit of Dr. Albert Schweitzer" (as translated from by Dr Schweitzer's interpreter), *The Silcoatian*, New Series No. 25 (December, 1935): 783-785.

Senesh, H., Piercy, M., Senesh, E., & Grossman, R. (2014). *Hannah Senesh: Her life and diary*. Strawberry Hills, NSW: ReadHowYouWant.

Shakespeare, William. *Henry V.* Act II, Scene 4,

Shermer, M. (2008, May 13). "The Brain is Not Modular: What fMRI Really Tells Us." *Scientific American*. Retrieved from http://www.sciam.com/article.cfm?id=a-new-phrenology&print=true

Smith, A. W. (2013). *Overcoming perfectionism: Finding the key to balance and self-acceptance*. Deerfield Beach, FL: Health Communications.

Soller, J. (2004). Cradles of Eminence 2nd Edition: Childhoods of More Than 700 Famous Men and Women. *Gifted and Talented International, 19*(2), 111-112. doi:10.1080/15332276.2004.11673046

Sternberg, R. J. (1988). *The triarchic mind: A new theory of human intelligence.* New York": Viking.

Sweatt, J. D. (2007). An Atomic Switch for Memory. *Cell, 129*(1), 23-24. doi:10.1016/j.cell.2007.03.021

Szyf, M. (2009a). Early life, the epigenome and human health. *Acta Paediatrica, 98*(7), 1082-1084. doi:10.1111/j.1651-2227.2009.01382.

Szyf, M. (2009b). Epigenetics, DNA methylation and chromatin modifying drugs. Annu. Rev. Pharmacol. Toxicol. 49, 243–263. 10.1146/annurev-pharmtox-061008-103102.

Teen Creates 'Sit with Us' App For Bullied Kids. (2016, September). Retrieved November 10, 2016, from http://www.npr.org/2016/09/09/493319114/teen-creates-sit-with-us-app-for-bullied-kids

Van Gemert, L. (2011, August). "Back to Basics." *Mensa Bulletin.* 26-29.

Van Gemert, L. (2014, August). The EF Gap. *Mensa Bulletin,* 22-25.

Vidmar, P. (1985, May). Pursuing Excellence. *Ensign,* 38.

Wells, N.M. & Evans, G.W. (2003). Nearby nature: A buffer of life stress among rural children. *Environment and Behavior,* (32) 6, pp775- 795.

Wansink, B., Just, D. R., Payne, C. R., & Klinger, M. Z. (2012). Attractive names sustain increased vegetable intake in schools. *Preventive Medicine, 55*(4), 330-332. doi:10.1016/j.ypmed.2012.07.012

Webb, J. T., Gore, J. L., Amend, E. R., & DeVries, A. R. (2007). *A parent's guide to gifted children.* Scottsdale, AZ; Great Potential Press.

Whitney, C. S., & Hirsch, G. (2007). *Love for learning: Motivation and the gifted child.* Scottsdale, AZ: Great Potential Press.

Willingham, D. (2009). *Why don't students like school?* San Francisco, CA: Jossey-Bass.

Wrosch, C., Scheier, M. F., Carver, C. S., & Schulz, R. (2003). The Importance of Goal Disengagement in Adaptive Self-Regulation: When

Giving Up is Beneficial. *Self and Identity, 2*(1), 1-20. doi:10.1080/15298860309021

Wrosch, C., Scheier, M. F., Miller, G. E., Schulz, R., & Carver, C. S. (2003). Adaptive Self-Regulation of Unattainable Goals: Goal Disengagement, Goal Reengagement, and Subjective Well-Being. *Personality and Social Psychology Bulletin, 29*(12), 1494-1508. doi:10.1177/0146167203256921

Zeidner, M., & Shani-Zinovich, I. (2011). Do academically gifted and nongifted students differ on the Big-Five and adaptive status? Some recent data and conclusions. *Personality & Individual Differences, 51*(5), 566-570. doi:10.1016/j.paid.2011.05.007

ABOUT THE AUTHOR

Lisa Van Gemert works with gifted youth, their parents, and educators around the world. Her passion for the gifted began when she was identified as gifted in her elementary school and saw how being in a class of all highly able students changed her entire educational experience. She began her career  in education as a teacher, and taught both elementary and high school, as well as homeschooling her own children while they lived in Germany for three years. Lisa was an administrator at a large high school before becoming the Youth & Education Ambassador for Mensa. She has authored the children's and teachers' guides to the National Book Festival for the Library of Congress and served as expert consultant to the *Lifetime* show "Child Genius" for two seasons.

Lisa received her B.A. *summa cum laude* from the University of Texas at Arlington, graduating from the Honors College. She also received her M.Ed.T. and did her graduate work in Educational Administration at the same institution. Currently, she writes and speaks about giftedness and advocates for gifted families and educators on her website, http://giftedguru.com and, with her colleague Ian Byrd, offers a community for educators of the gifted at http://giftedguild.com.

Lisa lives in Arlington, Texas, with her husband and golden retriever Brody, who is not gifted.

ENDNOTES

[1] Greenspon, T. (2007), p. 92.

[2] These different types of perfectionism are described more fully in the book *Letting Go of Perfect*, by Jill Adelson and Hope Wilson. Both authors are educators, and their views of the types of perfectionism reflect the ways perfectionism manifests itself in school settings.

[3] The Big Five model is a personality trait model that has grown in popularity over the past fifty years or so. It narrows personality traits from the thousands that exist in other models to only five broad categories: extraversion, agreeableness, conscientiousness, Neuroticism, Openness.

[4] An excellent resource to find books with characters showing perfectionism is *Some of My Best Friends Are Books: Guiding Gifted Readers from Preschool to High School*, by Judith Wynn Halsted. She provides a brief description of several hundred books, the issues that they deal with, and gives questions you can use to help promote insight and identification with the characters in the books. Similarly, several movies feature perfectionistic characters.

[5] Gifted children and adults tend to be particularly intense in almost everything they do—including in their self-talk—and that this can lead them to "catastrophizing" in their negative thinking and self-talk. This is described extensively in *A Parent's Guide to Gifted Children* by Webb, Gore, Amend, and DeVries (2007).

[6] Several books, such as *A Parent's Guide to Gifted Children*, by Webb, Gore, Amend, and DeVries (2007), or *Love for Learning: Motivation and the Gifted Child*, by Whitney and Hirsch (2007), can be quite helpful in sorting out why a child seems unmotivated, as well as providing practical strategies.

[7] The overexcitabilities, which are a key part of Dabrowski's theory, are explained well in the book *Living with Intensity*, by Daniels and Piechowski, (2008).

[8] Hewitt, Flett, Turnbull-Donovan, & Mikail (1991) separated perfectionism into types in measuring it with the Multidimensional Perfectionism Scale. The three types were self-oriented perfectionism (SOP) in which you impose the standards on yourself, socially prescribed perfectionism (SPP) in which you perceive that others are imposing standards on you, and other-prescribed perfectionism (OPP) in which there are standards imposed on you by others. Other articles that explore this idea include Affrunti and Woodruff-Borden, J. (2014) and Dunkley, Zuroff, & Blankstein (2003).

[9] Antony & Swinson (2009).

[10] One of the first papers to explore the idea of adaptive versus maladaptive perfectionism was Frost, Heimberg, Holt, Mattia & Neubauer (1993). It continues to be explored in recent research as well, including Moate, Gnilka, West & Bruns (2016), Gong, Fletcher, & Bolin (2015), and Affrunti & Woodruff-Borden, J. (2014).

[11] Smith (2013).

[12] Csikszentmihalyi, M. (2009).

[13] Galbraith & Delisle (2015), p. 64.

[14] Bluestein (2015), p. 254.

[15] You can read the current full diagnostic criteria for Autism Spectrum Disorder at https://www.autismspeaks.org/what-autism/diagnosis/dsm-5-diagnostic-criteria.

[16] American Psychiatric Association. (2013), pp. 678-679.

[17] American Psychiatric Association. (2013) pp. 678-679.

[18] Joanne Foster (2015), in her book *Not Now, Maybe Later*, makes this same important point.

[19] Partnoy, F. (2012), p. 150.

[20] Bronson & Merryman (2013).

[21] Adderholdt, Johnson & Levy (2015), p. 8.

[22] Kate Maupin (2014), in her book *Cheating, Dishonesty, and Manipulation: Why Bright Kids Do It*, explains this in much more detail.

[23] Kavaphēs & Dalven (1961), pp. 36-37.

[24] Fogg is the founder of Stanford's Persuasive Technology Lab, You can learn more about his theories at one of Dr. Fogg's numerous websites, such as http://bjfogg.com,

http://behaviormodel.org, and http://tinyhabits.com, as well as the website of the Stanford Persuasive Development Lab https://captology.stanford.edu.

[25] Knowles (1987), p. 196.

[26] Vidmar (1985), p. 38.

[27] Duckworth, Peterson, Matthews, & Kelly (2007).

[28] Two key studies on goal disengagement's role in psychological success include Wrosch, Scheier, Carver, & Schulz (2003) and Wrosch, Scheier, Miller, Schulz, & Carver (2003).

[29] Canfield, J., & Wells, H. C. (1976).

[30] You can read a summary of the American Association of University Women study, *Shortchanging Girls, Shortchanging America*, at http://www.aauw.org/files/2013/02/shortchanging-girls-shortchanging-america-executive-summary.pdf. This summary includes the statistics referred to in the chapter.

[31] http://www.girlscouts.org/content/dam/girlscouts-gsusa/forms-and-documents/about-girl-scouts/research/beauty_redefined_factsheet.pdf.

[32] Senesh, Piercy, Senesh, & Grossman. (2014), p. 62.

[33] Schweitzer (1935).

[34] http://www.willlourceyfrogs.com

[35] Learn more about World Wise Schools at https://www.peacecorps.gov/educators.

[36] Loans can be made around the world through http://kiva.org.

[37] Bluestein (2015).

[38] Neihart (2006).

[39] Ericsson, Krampe, & Tesch-Römer (1993)

[40] Gladwell (2008), p. 39.

[41] Chambliss (1989)

[42] Wansink, Just, Payne, & Klinger (2012).

[43] Peters (2013), pp.77-78.

[44] More information and resources on mental health are available at http://www.giftedguru.com/emotional-health, including a full list of mindfulness exercises that Patricia Bear, LPC has gathered.

[45] Greenspon & Samples (2002).

[46] Fitts & Posner (1967).

[47] Foer, J. (2011).

[48] Read more about Alex's Lemonade Stand at http://www.alexslemonade.org.

[49] Monk, Spicer, & Champagne (2012), Danchin, Charmantier, Campagne, Mesoudi, Pujol, and Blanchet (2011), and Champagne (2008).

[50] Some of the studies relevant to resiliency include: Szyf (2009a), Szyf (2009b), Bagot, van Hasselt, Champagne, Meaney, Krugers, & Joëls (2009), and Sweatt, J. D. (2007). A more detailed, yet still readable, analysis of the role of epigenetics on child development is from the *Early Experiences Can Alter Gene Expression and Affect Long-Term Development: Working Paper No. 10,* by the National Scientific Council on the Developing Child (2010).

[51] CASA (2010).

[52] The National Center on Addiction and Substance Abuse (CASA) found that teens who eat with their parents do better in school, have less mental stress, and are far less likely to abuse drugs or alcohol. They have released a number of studies over the past decade, all with similar findings.

[53] Ginsburg, Jablow, & Ginsburg (2011).

[54] Moore (2005) and Moore (2012).

[55] Bohanek, Marin, Fivush, & Duke (2006).

[56] The complete list of twenty questions can be seen at http://www.huffingtonpost.com/marshall-p-duke/the-stories-that-bind-us-b_2918975.html

[57] Sternberg (1989).

[58] This strategy is discussed in Canfield & Wells (1976).

[59] http://www.apa.org/helpcenter/resilience.aspx

[60] Bengtsson, Dolan, & Passingham (2011).

[61] Shermer (2008).

[62] Mental Health America (2006).

[63] Hofferth & Sandberg (1999). Read the full study at http://www.psc.isr.umich.edu/pubs/pdf/rr00-456.pdf.

[64] Hillman, Adams, & Whitelegg, J.(2000).

[65] Darley, J. M., & Batson, C. D. (1973).

[66] Wells & Evans (2003).

[67] Soller (2004) gives a summary, but the complete work is Goertzel, Goertzel, Goertzel, & Hansen (2004). *Cradles of Eminence: The Childhoods of More than 700 Famous Men and Women.*

[68] Fredricks, Flanagan, & Alfeld, C. J. (2010).

[69] Adderholdt, Johnson, & Levy (2015).

[70] Willingham (2009).

[71] Cooperrider & Srivastva (1987).

[72] Van Gemert (2014).

[73] Van Gemert (2014).

[74] Gnilka, Ashby, & Noble (2012).

[75] Dunkley, Zuroff, & Blankstein (2003).

[76] "Teen creates" (Hampton, 2016). http://www.npr.org/2016/09/09/493319114/teen-creates-sit-with-us-app-for-bullied-kids

[77] Ariely, Kamenica, & Prelec (2008).

[78] Duckworth, Kirby, Gollwitzer, & Oettingen (2013).

[79] These findings are from a meta-analysis done by Philip Babcock and Mindy Marks (2010) to look at time use in college students for the last 90 years.

[80] Sanders (1987).